PAM KRAUSS BOOKS/AVERY
NEW YORK

DOWNTIME

°DELICIOUSNESS AT HOME

NADINE LEVY REDZEPI

PHOTOGRAPHS BY DITTE ISAGER
STYLED BY CHRISTINE RUDOLPH

Pam Krauss Books / Avery
an imprint of Penguin Random House LLC
375 Hudson Street
New York, New York 10014

Most Avery books are available at special quantity discounts for bulk purchase for sales
promotions, premiums, fund-raising, and educational needs. Special books or book excerpts also
can be created to fit specific needs. For details, write SpecialMarkets@penguinrandomhouse.com.

ISBN 9780735216068

Printed in China
1 3 5 7 9 10 8 6 4 2

Book design by Ashley Tucker

The recipes contained in this book have been created for the ingredients and techniques indicated.
The publisher is not responsible for your specific health or allergy needs that may require
supervision. Nor is the publisher responsible for any adverse reactions you may have
to the recipes contained in the book, whether you follow them as written
or modify them to suit your personal dietary needs or tastes.

To my wonderful family, friends,
recipe testers, and everyone who has
been a part of making this book

CONTENTS

"Chef, we won't be needing you this evening, so you can head home."

This disorienting comment was directed at me many years ago, when Noma was just a handful of cooks who filled three-quarters of the dining room on a good night. If we did twenty covers at lunch, we'd be high-fiving one another.

"What? Is this a joke?" I said, not doing a very good job of hiding my irritation. "Dining room's actually full tonight." Besides that, this was a Saturday—I'm never off on Saturday—and the order came from a sous-chef, which puzzled me even more.

"No, seriously, you're going home, we're good," he affirmed, seconded by a chorus of encouraging glances from the rest of the team. I had no choice but to hop on my bike and see what was going on.

When I opened the door to our tiny one-bedroom apartment there were no kids around, just Nadine with a light sheen of sweat on her forehead, cooking. Pots and pans were sizzling away on the little gas burner, and steam was coming from every corner of the kitchen. In a Keyser Söze flash, my brain was flooded with images of her recent activities at the restaurant, whispers and meetings with my cooks that had struck me as somewhat sneaky at the time, though it had never occurred to me what she could possibly have in mind.

The joke was definitely on me, in the form of a five-course menu Nadine had been planning for months. She poured me a glass of wine. "Sit down, relax," she said. It began, I'll never forget, with a meticulously arranged platter of the season's vegetables, both raw and cooked, marinated in a luxurious and perfect truffle sauce. I still can't figure out how she made it, but I remember thinking to myself, "Man, that should be on the menu at Noma." As clever and observant as anyone I've ever met, Nadine had remembered a rare vacation we took to France and just how much we enjoyed eating crudités there. Now, for our first free night together in months, she had put her own spin on it. She followed this with a dish of potato skins more wonderful than any I've ever encountered. Usually, you're only able to get a handful to that paper-thin crispness while maintaining just the right amount of creamy potato layer, but she had managed to make every single one the ideal. She had also fashioned Brussels sprout leaves into little cups and filled each with a buttery fish roe sauce. I can't quite recall what came after—aside from lots of champagne and fits of laughter that almost hurt—but to this day, it's the greatest meal I've ever eaten.

It certainly wasn't the first time she had cooked for me. I met Nadine when she was nineteen, and in those early days, when we were just getting to know each other, it always amazed me to hear that she spent her nights at home cooking for herself. I always figured teenagers went for the typical cop-out of ordering in or meeting friends at a fast food joint. At best, they'd make themselves some buttered toast.

On one of our first dates, with no inside information about my likes or dislikes, she made us a dish of sautéed chicken livers with a sauce of tomatoes and chiles. Nadine wasn't totally happy with the end result, but I was thrilled: by some cosmic force she had chosen to make the one dish I had loved more than any other as a child. I wouldn't say that my family was poor, but when I was growing up there definitely wasn't a lot of money around. Most nights we ate a hearty stew of beans, and when we did eat meat, it was usually an off-cut. My mother, a Dane, would find a frozen, somewhat neglected bag of chicken livers in the supermarket and cook it with flavors that my father, from the former Yugoslavia, enjoyed: mushrooms, the versatile seasoning Vegeta, and—you guessed it—tomatoes and chiles. Nadine served it to me with pasta noodles, just as my mother had when I was a kid.

I don't for one second mind sounding silly, like a story from a cheap teenager's magazine, when I say that was the evening I realized that for each of us, there is someone out there who couldn't be with anyone else, and I had been lucky enough to find mine. From that day forward, she and I were it. Thank god for chicken livers.

All of this is to say that Nadine, without ever intending it, reminded me of the values a cook can sometimes forget when they've spent most of their young career as a mercenary in adrenaline-fueled kitchens. If I hadn't seen her channeling all of her best intentions into making someone happy,

I don't think Noma would have ended up where it has. Her lack of ego and generosity of spirit showed me, and the chefs whom she would ask for tips or would cook for on their nights off, why people gather around a table.

Lately, all of this has become even more obvious as we raise our three daughters. In our home, there is always cooking going on. It's not only a comfort we can count on, it's a kind of electrical current that runs through the family and keeps it going and together. Noma is a home for everyone, of course—so many kids have grown up there—but the kitchen in our house is this family's heart. As of this writing, our middle one, Genta, has learned to bake bread.

You may feel it's hard, or even impossible, to cook one meal a day when you have to make a living in the modern world. I see your point (in a way, even I can't do that for my kids!). Yet in this book I see someone who, by creating habits just like people do with exercise, has made the act of cooking effortless and endlessly generative. There is so much you can do if you simply begin to try.

As I write about what Nadine has created for our family, which she is now sharing in this book, I think about how dumb I must have sounded all of those times when I was young and would talk about restaurant chefs like they were famous athletes, saying "Man, that guy can cook!" or "They only had two cooks on the line and were still able to bang out all those covers." These days, I'm much more in awe of the parents and grandparents and caretakers who stroll up and down the grocery store aisle several times a week, trying to come up with something that the kids won't reject after they put it in their mouths.

Of these, Nadine is the best I know.

INTRODUCTION

You could say my whole life revolves around cooking and eating. It's not only the family business—both my husband, René, and I work at Noma, the restaurant he co-founded—it's what helps me relax and feel connected to home and family. It is the thing I look forward to doing every day. As far as I'm concerned, there *is* no downtime without something to eat or drink, and when I get into that cooking mode, that's when my real downtime begins.

It's always been this way for me. I grew up watching my mother cook and when I discovered food programs on television, duplicating the dishes I saw or trying to re-create things I'd tasted on vacations became a passion.

Now that our family and business have grown to include three young daughters, three restaurants, and a nonprofit foundation dedicated to creating new ways for chefs to explore important food issues, I treasure our downtime more than ever. I try to make space for this daily ritual no matter what else is going on in our lives—and whoever might be joining us at the table.

At Noma, the office, test kitchen, and staff dining area all share one big open room on the floor above the restaurant and as I work, the scents that flow from the test kitchen cause my mind to drift here and there, triggering thoughts of different flavor combinations and what we might have for dinner that night.

I go food shopping pretty much every day and I make a point of using that period to get my head out of work and into family time. I love going to the market and getting a cappuccino to go, saying hello to people I know as I walk from stand to stand, noticing how the fruit and vegetables change with the seasons.

I usually arrive without a concrete plan of what to buy because I know that when I am hungry I want to eat *everything* and ideas for meals will come very quickly. I start imagining how delicious it would be to serve this with that and add a little of another thing—all the while thinking how my kids will like it and what stories they will tell me while I am cooking.

I am never alone in the kitchen. Our dining space, kitchen, and living room are all one big room, which makes the kitchen the natural gathering place. Whether we have friends over for dinner or it is just us cooking with music playing in the background, it is always the same: my older daughters, Arwen and Genta, help peel vegetables, rinse greens for a salad, and fight over who made the vinaigrette yesterday and who gets to make it today. My mother changes the music continuously while our youngest daughter, Ro, plays on the floor or joins in by sticking her hands and fingers into

everything. (If there happens to be butter on the table, she will eat as much of it as she can if I don't keep an eye on her.) This warm togetherness adds an extra dimension of *hygge,* as we Danes call it, to the ritual of preparing a family meal that makes it all the more pleasurable.

I've learned to be flexible about dinner because I never really know how many we will be. When people drop by unexpectedly, one of the kids has a friend over, or the spouse of someone from the restaurant stops in for a visit, they are always welcome to join us at the table. Sometimes I just need to slice the meat a bit thinner, add more vegetables to the sauce, or make a bigger salad but we can always accomodate one or two more. And though I do think about what the kids will like to eat, I don't cook a separate meal

Cook for guests as you would for family. Treat your family like company.

for them; as much as I love cooking I don't want to cook two dinners every day. I would rather spend that extra time and effort on making a bigger dinner for everyone, adding a special dessert or a more elaborate starter.

On weekends we usually entertain at least once or twice, but because we keep it comfortable and relaxed, having guests doesn't feel like "work." Everyone gathers at the island, eating something tasty, helping with the prep if they want, having some wine, listening to music, and before you know it there's a great buzz in the room. It makes you more relaxed as a host having all these people being part of preparing dinner because it takes some pressure off your shoulders, instead of it being your responsibility to get dinner on the table for everyone.

One of the many things that I have learned from working at Noma and being with René is understanding what makes me immediately feel welcome and at ease. By

learning this about yourself, you become better at creating the atmosphere you want in your own home when you have guests over. If you are at ease, everyone else will be, too.

When we entertain, I rarely get fancy and elaborate; rather our guests come and join us for a family meal. I've served roast chicken to Daniel Patterson, broth with rice and eggs to Matty Mathieson, and roasted ribs and sweet potatoes to David Chang. I'm often asked if it's intimidating to cook for professional chefs, and I'll admit I was nervous the first time I cooked for René, but I soon realized that chefs spend so much time cooking for other people that they are just happy and appreciative when someone cooks for them! (And they are handy in the kitchen as sous-chefs.) They don't expect a fancy meal with foams and garnishes, they just want well-flavored food made with good-quality ingredients—exactly what you'd make for your own family. On the other hand, it's fun to surprise your family with something a bit sophisticated and extravagant for no special reason. On those days I'll slip a bit of truffle puree into the stuffing for a pork roast, or make a giant macaron filled with whipped cream and a thin layer of cake for dessert.

I take great pleasure in cooking a proper evening meal every day, not just something quick and lazy even if it is "just" us. *Downtime* is a collection of the recipes I make most often for family, friends, and everyone else in between. It's an eclectic mix of comfort food dishes—some of which I have been eating and preparing since childhood—upgraded with what I've learned about ingredients, flavor, and kitchen technique. Most important, it's a book of the family traditions I mean to pass along to my kids, and that I hope can become part of your daily ritual as well.

HOW TO USE THIS BOOK

The book is divided into three simple sections: Starters, Mains, and Desserts, but with the exception of the desserts (or most of them) those distinctions are largely semantic. I often serve traditional breakfast foods like omelets and porridges for dinner, and I would happily make a breakfast of the chicken broth with soy egg or serve the braised leeks appetizer for a light summer entrée. Many of my favorite starters can double as party food on a buffet or be plated up individually as the first course of a more formal meal. Most of the desserts are equally fantastic for big celebrations and afterschool treats. Again, it's all about blurring the distinction between family food and special occasions. It is kind of like my mother's advice on buying a gift: get them something that you would want yourself. If you cook something you want to eat, you can't really go wrong.

This is not a restaurant cookbook, and with a few exceptions, most of the food I serve at home is simple, flavorful comfort food. That said, working at Noma and being married to its chef has given me the incredible opportunity to do lots of traveling, to dine at wonderful restaurants, and become good friends with some of the world's best chefs. Along the way I have picked up a few techniques and tricks that I have incorporated into my cooking at home even while keeping things simple and practical.

I've heard many people say they would never serve something they hadn't made before for company, but that's not really my philosophy. When people come to the house, it's loose and comfortable; they don't think they're going to a restaurant. I think it's fun to try something new and have everyone give you their feedback. Mistakes are a learning process, and from working at Noma I've learned that many of the best things on the menu started out as an experiment gone wrong in the test kitchen!

You don't need to have chef-level skills to make any of the dishes in this book, though some of these recipes will make you look like a culinary superstar, turning out plates that wouldn't be out of place in a fine restaurant. To ensure success, I've added tips and notes throughout that I hope will make you feel like you are being walked through the recipes as you cook. Once you have made them a few times you probably won't need these pointers, but until then, I have your back.

A few more rules that I live by:

Build On What You Know

You'll see some recurring themes throughout this book, basic templates that I build on to create layers of flavor and sophistication from components I love and make often. Although some of these dishes share a basic procedure, the outcomes look and taste very different. The beauty is that you aren't reinventing the wheel every time you step in the kitchen; you'll soon develop a level of comfort with these dishes and find that they come together very quickly as you mix and match components you have mastered previously. Once they are second nature, you can create complexity by bringing in more exotic elements like fish roe, a cured egg yolk, or prunes macerated

in brandy. It's a smart, easy way to make something simple seem really polished and professional. And rest assured, no one will accuse you of repeating yourself.

Don't Fear Fat

Another thing that working so close to a restaurant kitchen has taught me is that fat can really bring out the flavor in a vegetable or piece of protein. Butter basting is one of the first things I picked up when I started working at Noma. I noticed that the chef in charge of the hot section was cooking a piece of musk ox in more butter than I had ever seen in a pan, spooning the hot fat over the meat again and again. He explained it makes most things juicier and can enhance the flavor of almost anything. Now I almost always give pan-fried foods a bath of butter right at the end, and even drop a few tablespoons of butter into the cooking water for vegetables. And for creating incomparable crispness and sealing in flavor, nothing beats deep-frying; what would life be without chips or eggplant parm?

Lastly, Observe Your Food

Just like eating, cooking should engage all of your senses. Learning to notice and interpret the signs and signals food gives you as it goes through the cooking process is far more important than sticking to timing stated in a recipe. You'll know your meat is ready to be turned in the pan because it looks delicious and appetizing; when your clams pop open or your roasted sweet potatoes start to ooze caramelized sugars, you'll know they are done to perfection, no matter what the clock says.

THE DOWNTIME PANTRY

At home there are no rules about what ingredients you can use or which cuisines you should cook. Be as eclectic and experimental as you want, mixing dishes from different countries. Having spent my early childhood in Portugal and England and my summers in France before moving to Denmark when I was six, I don't even think about crossing borders in the kitchen.

As a family we've had the opportunity to travel extensively, and whenever we do we absorb a bit of the local food culture. I always take something back home from these travels that becomes a permanent part of the way I cook, from the sticky rice I serve with just about everything to a cooling frozen avocado pie that evokes vacations in Mexico.

The only real rule I follow is that I want all of my ingredients to be of the very highest quality. I strongly believe the better the produce, the better the food. Much of the food produced in Denmark is organic, and it means a lot to me that I am cooking food for my children and friends that is produced responsibly. I bike all over town to pick up just one thing here and another from a store three miles away. I have one favorite butcher for pork and beef and another butcher for chicken, duck breast, and pâté. Lucky for me, all of these places are within walking distance of one another.

When you have good produce full of flavor, you need less seasoning. I try not to use too much salt in my cooking and I don't automatically salt the water when I boil vegetables or meat or fish before I pan-sear them. I do use coarse sea salt for pasta water and a finer sea salt for some baking recipes, but for almost all other purposes I prefer the clean taste of a flaky sea salt such as Maldon. I like the variation in the size of the flakes and, to me, it both looks and tastes better when you season your food right before serving.

When I was learning to cook, I always used salt and pepper together, but now I think of pepper more as a spice, as it does have a very strong flavor. In something like a pasta carbonara, it makes the whole dish, but it can be too assertive in other dishes, so I add it thoughtfully and with care.

That said, I do encourage people to season their food to their own liking and always set freshly ground pepper, flaky salt, olive oil, and a small bowl of extra chopped herbs on the table. This lets friends and the kids try something in a different way and I like to watch how people add such different amounts of seasoning on their food. I'm interested to see that my children don't want pepper on their fish, but they do on their steak. I love that they think about the flavor and know how they like their food.

The dairy in Denmark is amazing, and for the richest desserts I love to use double cream, which has a fat content of more than 45 percent as opposed to **heavy cream's** 35 percent, and tastes naturally sweet. As it is not widely available in the United States, be sure to use the freshest organic cream you can find, preferably not ultra-pasteurized. **Crème fraîche** is one of the best things in the world, thick, creamy, and acidic. Two essential staples in our household are eggs and butter. At any given time I have a kilo of butter on hand (that's more than two pounds) and we use as many as six dozen fresh organic **eggs** per week between breakfasts, baking, and all the other amazing ways these versatile protein sources can be cooked. For almost every purpose, including baking, I prefer **salted butter**, and the recipes in this book indicate that. If you strongly prefer to use unsalted butter, you may need to season your food more assertively along the way.

We consume fish and **meat** consciously and in moderate portions, though we are by no means vegetarian. I like using cuts such as lamb shoulder, pork cheeks, and pork belly that you won't necessarily find packaged in the meat case of your supermarket. These cuts are often cheaper than "prime" cuts like steak and chops because they take longer to cook. They may require more time in the pan, but they do not require much actual cooking from *you*. Better still, they are rich and full of flavor and can serve a lot of people. Get friendly with the butchers; they can often special order less-common cuts for you if you call ahead. And learn to love sustainable shellfish like mussels and clams.

I have a pretty well-stocked pantry, and it's comforting to know that when I get up and can tell it's going to be a day I spend in my pajamas, I can always make a meal without leaving the house. I always have three types of **oil** on hand for different uses: A neutral-flavored oil like canola or grapeseed is best for frying or sautéing and making mayonnaise. For dressings, marinades, and to add body to sauces I use a good- but not best-quality olive oil. And I reserve a really good tasty olive oil to drizzle over salads, meat, or fish at the table. Other pantry ingredients we're never without are good-quality dried **pastas**; **organic canned tomatoes and beans**; canned fish, like **anchovies** and **sardines**; and preserved **truffles**. I serve **sticky rice**, also known as glutinous rice, four or five times a week and when I make it I always deliberately cook enough for leftovers because the girls love it in their lunch boxes and it's so easy to turn into a fast meal by adding bits of leftover cooked vegetables, meat, or eggs.

THE BAKING PANTRY

Nuts and nut flours—almond, hazelnut, and walnuts in particular—show up in so many of my desserts, and **almond paste**, similar to marzipan but with a higher percentage of nuts and less sugar, is found in the baking section of most grocery stores. Fresh **vanilla beans** are an ingredient I insist on; I would never use vanilla extract, especially when it's the primary flavor, as it simply doesn't taste the same as the beans. For most recipes **raw sugar**, also called turbinado, is my standby. I share the Scandinavian obsession with licorice and a few of the dessert recipes in this book call for **licorice powder** as an optional addition. You may not be able to get it in your local supermarket, but you can order it online and it can be stored like any dried spice. Another favorite dessert flavoring is freeze-dried **fruit powders**. Freeze-dried fruits are becoming more widely available in the snack aisle; crush them to a powder with a mortar and pestle or in the food processor.

TOOLS AND EQUIPMENT

You might expect the home kitchen of a chef and his family to be tricked out with space-age appliances and all the latest high-end gadgets, but I've always believed you don't need a ton of expensive equipment to make great food. I recently ate at a friend's house and he proudly served a steak that he had cooked in a sous vide machine then seared with a kitchen torch. I appreciated the effort, but to me the steak would have had so much more flavor if he had just cooked it in a pan.

Until quite recently we have always lived in rental apartments, with average appliances and not a lot of storage space for kitchen gear; I only bought my first food processor last year! In our current home we had the opportunity to design the kitchen with a carpenter so the setup is great, but it is still just a home kitchen. I have a very good oven, a few small appliances, and a handful of simple tools. The list below comprises the items I rely on most often, just about everything you will need to make any of the recipes in this book.

Sharp knives and a sharpening steel: I probably don't have my knives professionally sharpened as often as I should, but I do make sure to give them a few swipes with the steel before each use to straighten out any minor nicks in the edge, which also prolongs the time between real sharpenings.

Food processor and blender: For most jobs you can use one or the other, so it's not absolutely necessary to own both. That said, I tend to use the food processor for things like pulverizing nut brittle or grinding nuts to make flour. For pureeing liquids and soups, I use the blender.

Electric mixer: If you are a baker, there is nothing more indispensable for beating air into meringues and creating smooth batters and frostings. If you have a stand mixer with changeable beaters, so much the better, but if you have only a hand mixer, you can still make any of these recipes; you just may need to beat a little longer. **Whisks** won't take the place of a mixer but you'll want one for making mayos, butter sauces, and vinaigrettes.

Skillets: Ideally you'll have a heavy, straight-sided skillet for searing meats, making pasta sauces, and shallow-frying, plus another nonstick sauté pan for cooking delicate fish and making omelets.

Other pots and pans: I use my heavy **Dutch oven** more than just about any other pot in the kitchen. It is great for braising, simmering soups, and making curries, and because it retains heat well it helps control the temperature for deep-frying. In a pinch you can use if for making pasta and stocks if you don't have room for a larger **stockpot**.

Rimmed baking sheets, also known as half sheet pans, are useful for so many things, from roasting spare ribs to toasting bread crumbs and baking cookies. You should have at least two; four is better.

Skimmers and strainers: I deep-fry a lot and a shallow basket, long-handled skimmer, also called a spider, is the best for lifting fried food from the hot oil as well as scooping pasta and vegetables out of boiling water. Wire mesh sieves are handy for sifting flours and straining stocks, and making silky-smooth mashed potatoes. Buy a large one and a smaller one if you have room for both as well as a colander for draining pasta, rinsing greens, and much more.

Tongs, both metal and rubber tipped, rubber spatulas, and a long-handled spoon for basting.

A box grater or Microplane rasp for zesting citrus and shredding cheese.

Japanese mandolin/V-slicer: These don't need to be expensive. Mine is plastic and works just as well as the high-end metal versions. Essential if you are serious about making potato chips, and I am!

Parchment paper simplifies baking (and baking cleanup).

A kitchen scale for measuring chocolate and weighing cheese.

A kitchen timer to ensure perfectly hard-boiled eggs.

Instant-read thermometers are indispensable for roasted foods. A candy thermometer is necessary for cooking certain confections.

Last, if you find yourself making rice and ice cream as often as I do, you might want to invest in a countertop rice cooker and an inexpensive ice cream maker. If you have a stand mixer, you can buy an attachment that lets the mixer do the churning, but even a simple crank version with a liner you chill in the freezer does the job.

A FINAL NOTE

Preparing a meal doesn't end in the kitchen. I believe food tastes better on beautiful plates, and I collect ceramics and unique serving pieces obsessively. I have very few matching sets of china, it's all very mix-and-match and much of it picked up on our travels. I choose things based on size, shape, and what inspires me. When I see a beautiful plate, I immediately start to imagine what I could make to serve on it. In general, I think very large plates are a bad idea. You shouldn't have to load the plate up to make it look full.

STARTERS

The large island at the heart of our kitchen is also at the center of most meals I share with friends and family. When we have people over for dinner, instead of preparing very much before they show up, I do most of the cooking once they are here. I usually delegate small tasks to people as they arrive, which allows them to join in on the fun rather than waiting awkwardly at the table. Within a few minutes, everyone is peeling, chopping, and enjoying a glass of wine while my mom controls the music from her favorite chair and our girls climb on stools to watch and chat with the visitors. There's a wonderful buzz at the island, and it already feels like a party.

Rather than calling everyone to the table for a plated first course, I almost always start off dinners with some kind of finger food. While people are still busy in the kitchen I like to set out a platter of warm, homemade potato chips with a savory dip, or cups of perfect poached eggs served with crisply cooked spears of asparagus to poke into the yolks. Grilled or fried toasts, topped with something light but delicious, are satisfying but not too filling. I even consider steamed clams finger food—when you pick one up and slurp the meat right from the shell you get a delicious bit of sauce with every bite. Letting the cooking and the meal blend together this way creates a lovely, casual vibe that encourages guests to relax and feel at home. It also allows me to finish the main course without missing out on any of the conversation.

BEGIN WITH A POTATO

HOMEMADE POTATO CHIPS
WITH ANCHOVY HUMMUS

SERVES 4

You may be wondering why I bother making either, much less both, of these when there are good commercial products in every market. Really, it comes down to flavor and quality. Whenever I use store-bought hummus I end up blending and tasting and seasoning it so much I finally realized I might as well make it from scratch. Potato chips are my biggest weakness— I will take a handful of chips over a candy bar any day and I feel really good about giving homemade snack foods like these to my kids or company, because I know exactly what's gone into them. If you have a mandoline or V-slicer, these chips are so easy to make, and sooo good.

POTATO CHIPS

Baking potatoes	2
Fine sea salt	1 teaspoon
Canola oil	1 quart (960 ml), as needed

ANCHOVY HUMMUS

Chickpeas	1 (15-ounce/420 g) can, preferably organic
Garlic clove	1
Extra-virgin olive oil	¼ cup (60 ml), plus more for drizzling
Plain (whole or low-fat) yogurt	1 tablespoon
Tahini	1 tablespoon
Fresh lemon juice	2 teaspoons
Anchovy fillets in olive oil	8 to 12
Cumin seeds	
Smoked paprika	For garnish

1. **Make the potato chips:** Scrub the potatoes and pat dry. With a mandoline or V-slicer, finely slice the potatoes into chips. The slices should be as close to paper-thin as possible, but not fragile.

   It may take some practice to get the thickness right. If the slices are too thin, they will curl and be too fragile. If too thick, they will burn before they become crisp.

recipe continues ▸

2. Spread out a long row of paper towels. Lay the potato slices on the paper, sprinkle evenly with salt, and top with another layer of paper towels. Let them stand for about 15 minutes to draw out the water.

   This part is very important! Damp potatoes will make the oil splatter.

3. Pour enough oil into a large saucepan to come halfway up the sides and heat it over medium heat until it is shimmering. Lay out another row of fresh paper towels for draining the fried chips.

   Use the end of a wooden spoon to check if the oil is at the correct temperature—if the oil starts to bubble around the spoon, the oil is hot enough.

4. Start by adding just two potato slices to the hot oil. When they are golden brown around the edges, use a slotted spoon to turn them over. Cook for another 30 seconds or until the chip is light brown. Drain on the paper towels. Continue frying the potatoes a few at a time, allowing the oil to return to the proper temperature before adding more.

   Once you get the hang of frying the chips you can cook more at a time, but don't add so many that you crowd the pan. The oil temperature will drop and they won't get crisp.

5. **Make the hummus:** Drain and rinse the chickpeas. Crush the garlic clove with the flat side of your knife and discard the papery skin. With the machine running, add the garlic clove through the feed tube of a food processor to mince the garlic. Add the chickpeas, ¼ cup (60 ml) oil, the yogurt, tahini, and lemon juice and process until smooth. Add the anchovies and purée.

   You should be able to taste the anchovies, but if they come across too strongly for you, add a little more yogurt and olive oil to balance the flavor.

6. Use a mortar and pestle or the bottom of a heavy saucepan to crush the cumin seeds.

7. Put the hummus in a serving bowl, drizzle with olive oil, and sprinkle with the crushed cumin and the smoked paprika. Serve the chips with the hummus.

If you don't own a mandoline or V-slicer yet, here is your excuse to buy one, because otherwise it's hard to make your chips thin or uniform enough to cook properly. These slicers are not expensive and will come in handy for many things, like the shaved cauliflower on page 86. But even if you never use it for any other purpose than making potato chips (or the sweet potato chips on page 35), the investment will be worth it, because these chips are so addictive and so versatile.

CHIPS WITH SALMON TARTARE

SERVES 8

This is a very forgiving tartare for people who are not sure they enjoy raw fish. It combines minced fresh salmon and smoked salmon, which, along with the vegetables, gives it a range of textures: soft, chewy, and crunchy. For this, I prefer hot-smoked salmon, which is drier and flakier and has a distinctly smokier flavor than the cold smoked salmon you eat with bagels, but either will work. Buy the best, freshest wild salmon you can here; you can never be certain about the conditions the fish are raised in with farmed salmon.

Cucumber	½
Fine sea salt	2 teaspoons, plus more to taste
Shallot	1 small
Cornichons	12
Fresh chives	30 blades
Fresh dill	30 sprigs
Skinless fresh salmon fillet	8 ounces (225 g)
Hot-smoked salmon fillets	8 ounces (225 g)
Crème fraîche	1 cup (225 ml), as needed
Fresh lemon juice	2 teaspoons, or to taste
Freshly ground black pepper	
Potato chips or crostini	For serving

1. Peel the cucumber. Cut it in half lengthwise and use a spoon to scrape out the seeds. Cut the cucumber lengthwise into strips about ¼ inch (6 mm) thick. Cut the strips crosswise into ¼-inch (6-mm) pieces. Toss with the 2 teaspoons of salt in a colander. Let drain for 30 minutes. Rinse well and pat dry with a tea towel.

    Salting the cucumber draws out its moisture so the dip won't be watery.

2. Peel and finely chop the shallot and put it in a large bowl with the cucumber. Now, finely chop the cornichons and add them to the bowl. Finely chop the

recipe continues ▸

chives and dill (you want about ¼ cup/20 g of each) and add to the bowl. Mix gently to combine.

3. Place the fresh salmon on your cutting board and run your fingers over the flesh side to detect the protruding ends of any thin white pin bones. Use your fingers or heavy tweezers to pull out and discard the bones. With a very sharp knife, cut the fish into thin strips and then cut the strips crosswise into small pieces. Mince the cubes as finely as you can. It's okay if the pieces are not all the same size but some bits should be minced almost to a mush. Cut the smoked salmon into very small pieces.

4. Add both kinds of salmon to the bowl and mix again. Gently stir in the crème fraîche. Add the 2 teaspoons lemon juice. Season to taste with salt and pepper.

   If you mix the crème fraîche too vigorously, it will become runny—it should remain thick and creamy.

5. Taste the tartare to see if you want to add more herbs or cornichons, or lemon juice for more acidity.

6. Transfer the spread to a serving bowl and serve, surrounded by the chips.

PANTRY CROSTINI

Serve the spread on small bread toasts for a more substantial bite. Whenever I have a leftover piece of baguette, I slice it thinly and toast the slices to serve with dips or snacks, or to drop into soups like croutons.

   You don't need a baking sheet to toast the bread. If you put them directly on the oven rack, the hot air will circulate around the slices and toast them without the need for turning. Just place the slices directly on the oven rack in a preheated 350°F (180°C) oven and toast for 10 to 15 minutes. Store in an airtight container for 2 weeks or freeze for 1 month.

SWEET POTATO CHIPS
WITH BLACK BEAN DIP

SERVES 4 TO 6

*Can you tell I love chips and dips? To me, they are such a nice, simple-yet-rich
thing to serve before a more substantial meal. They won't fill you up, but the
earthy dip and warmly spiced chips will keep your taste buds entertained.*

*Once you realize how easy it is to make your own potato chips, you'll realize that potatoes
are just one possibility: you can make chips from many starchy vegetables, including
carrots, beets, and, of course, sweet potatoes. Just about any kind of sweet potato works,
but for me, the maroon-skinned, white-fleshed Japanese sweet potatoes are the very best.
They have a flavor and texture something like a roasted chestnut, and because they
are starchier than the orange-fleshed varieties they fry up extra-crisp and don't seem
to curl as much. If you have time to cook black beans from scratch, that's great, but if
you buy canned, as I usually do, look for an organic brand. They just taste better.*

BLACK BEAN DIP

Canned black beans, preferably organic	1¼ cups (200 g)
Garlic cloves	2 small
Shallot	1 small
Cherry tomatoes	4
Chicken broth, melted butter, or olive oil	1 tablespoon, or as needed
Fine sea salt	
Fresh lemon juice	1 to 2 teaspoons
Fresh cilantro	12 sprigs
Extra-virgin olive oil	For serving

SWEET POTATO CHIPS

Sweet potatoes, preferably Japanese	2 medium
Fine sea salt	1 teaspoon
Canola oil, for deep-frying	1 quart (960 ml), as needed
Garam masala	1 to 2 teaspoons

recipe continues ▸

1. **Make the dip:** Rinse the beans under cold running water and drain them well. Crush the garlic cloves with the flat side of your knife and discard the papery skins. Peel the shallot. With the machine running, drop the shallot and garlic through the food tube of a food processor to mince them. Halve the cherry tomatoes and add them and the beans to the food processor. Pulse to chop. With the machine running, add the broth and purée. Season to taste with salt and lemon juice.

    If your beans are not very tender, you may need to add a bit more broth to get the dip nice and smooth. Add just a bit at a time; the only way to save a runny dip is to add more beans.

2. **Make the sweet potato chips:** Scrub the potatoes and pat dry. Use a mandoline, V-slicer, or very sharp knife to slice the potatoes almost paper-thin.

    The potato slices should be very thin but not fragile. If the slices are too fine, they will curl up in the hot oil. If too thick, they will burn before they become crisp.

3. Spread the potato slices on a double thickness of paper towels. Sprinkle the slices evenly with the salt and top with another layer of paper towels. Let them stand for about 20 minutes to draw out water from the potatoes.

    Don't skip this step! If the potato slices are too damp, the hot oil will splatter when you add them and they will become crispy only around the edges.

4. Pour enough oil to come halfway up the sides of a large saucepan and heat over medium heat until the oil is shimmering. To check the oil temperature, dip the end of a wooden spoon in the oil. When the oil starts to bubble around the spoon, it is hot enough.

5. Lay out another row of fresh paper near the stove. Slide two slices of potatoes into the hot oil. When they are golden brown around the edges, use a slotted spoon to turn them over and cook for another 30 seconds, until they are light brown all over. Use metal tongs to transfer them to the dry paper towels. Continue frying the potatoes a few at a time, allowing the oil to return to the proper temperature before adding more.

    Once you get the hang of frying the chips, you can cook more at a time, but don't add so many that you crowd the pan. The oil temperature will drop and they won't get crisp. If some of the chips are not quite as crispy as you would like, just put them back in the hot oil and fry a bit longer.

recipe continues ▸

6. Place the garam masala in a small sieve and sift it evenly over the hot chips. Let cool completely, then mound the chips in a bowl.

7. Coarsely chop the cilantro. Put the bean dip in a serving bowl, drizzle with olive oil, and sprinkle with the cilantro. Serve with the chips.

CONGRATULATIONS: YOU CAN MAKE SPICED CHIPS

With or without a dip, boldly seasoned chips are everyone's favorite snack. Always season the chips while they are hot, as it will help the flavorings cling better. Customize yours with your favorite flavors from around the world. Indiam garam masala, a blend of spices including cumin and chile, is a good choice. Here are some other ideas:

• Za'atar (a Lebanese mix of oregano, sesame, and more)
• Ras el hanout (a Moroccan blend of sweet and hot spices)
• Truffle salt
• Finely grated Parmigiano cheese and black pepper

POTATO SKINS WITH SALMON ROE

SERVES 6

It's not complicated to make these wonderful, perfect little mouthfuls, but there are a few steps involved. The payoff is huge, though, because they look so professional, and once you've mastered the technique you'll see how easy it is to dress the little potato cups up or down. If you have leftover tiny boiled potatoes, this is the perfect way to use them, but don't skip the baking step (just reduce the baking time to about 10 minutes); baking dries out the skins so they can get really crisp when you fry them. I like to use Yukon Gold potatoes, but any thin-skinned baby potato will work. And please don't waste the scooped-out potato flesh. That's actually how I came up with the cured-egg appetizer on page 47, but you could also mix it with an egg yolk for potato pancakes, or just reheat it with a bit of milk to accompany the breaded fish on page 183. I love this kind of kitchen recycling!

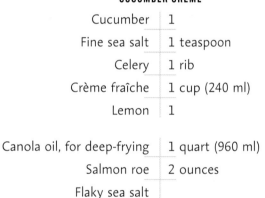

Baby potatoes	12, such as Yukon Golds

CUCUMBER CRÈME

Cucumber	1
Fine sea salt	1 teaspoon
Celery	1 rib
Crème fraîche	1 cup (240 ml)
Lemon	1
Canola oil, for deep-frying	1 quart (960 ml)
Salmon roe	2 ounces
Flaky sea salt	

1. **Prepare the potato skins:** Preheat the oven to 400°F (200°C). Spread the potatoes in a single layer on a large, rimmed baking sheet. Pierce each potato a few times with a fork. Bake until the potatoes are barely tender when pierced with the tip of a small knife, 30 to 40 minutes. Let the potatoes cool while you make the cucumber crème.

recipe continues ▶

2. Peel the cucumber, cut it in half lengthwise, and scoop out the seeds with the tip of a spoon. Cut the cucumber into very small dice (less than ⅛ inch/ 3 mm). Toss with about ½ teaspoon fine sea salt in a colander and let drain for 30 minutes. Rinse and pat dry with paper towels.

   Removing the seeds and salting the cuke help keep your crème from being watery.

3. Use a vegetable peeler to strip off and discard the celery strings. Cut the celery into long, thin strips, then cut them crosswise into small dice. Mix the crème fraîche, cucumber, and celery in a small bowl. Grate the zest of the lemon and add half to the cucumber sauce; reserve the rest for garnish. Cover and refrigerate separately.

   Do not stir the crème too much, or it will thin out.

4. Using a sharp knife, cut the cooled potatoes in half, being careful not to rip the skins. Use a teaspoon to scoop out most of the flesh, leaving shell about ⅛ inch (3 mm) thick.

5. **Fry the potato cups:** Pour enough oil into a medium saucepan to come halfway up the sides and heat it over medium heat until it is shimmering.

   Test the temperature of the oil with the end of a wooden spoon. When the oil is hot enough, bubbles will rise around the handle.

6. Line a baking sheet with paper towels and place it near the stove. Add a few potato cups to the hot oil, pushing them under the surface with a slotted spoon so the oil fills the cups and pulls them down into the oil. Fry until the potato skins are golden brown around their perimeters, about 2 minutes. Using the slotted spoon, transfer the skins to the baking sheet to drain. Repeat with the remaining potato cups.

   Once you get a feeling for how long these will take to cook, you can add more to the pot at a time. Be sure to let the oil get hot again between batches.

7. To serve, use a small spoon to fill the potato peels with the crème. Top each with a bit of the salmon roe. Arrange on a big platter and sprinkle with the reserved lemon zest and flaky sea salt.

BRUSSELS SPROUTS AND POTATO CUPS WITH BEURRE BLANC SAUCE AND ROE

SERVES 4 TO 6

Remember how I said you could dress the little potato cups on page 39 up or down? Here, they get the full black-tie treatment, with a soigné beurre blanc sauce, bright green Brussels sprout leaves, and a bit of decadent fish roe. I love the way the sprout leaves and potato skins cup the delicious sauce. I served this as part of a five-course tasting menu I prepared for René, and it was the ideal light yet elegant way to start an important meal. Here in Denmark fish markets often carry several different types of fresh roe, and when it is in season we eat it on and off with everything all day long. I've called for whitefish roe here because I like its pale golden color but trout roe or any type of caviar you can afford would be great, too. Just avoid the preserved lumpfish roe in shelf-stable jars, as it will be too salty and sharp.

Baby Yukon Gold potatoes	16
Brussels sprouts	2 (10-ounce/280-g) containers
Canola oil, for deep-frying	1 quart (960 ml), as needed

BEURRE BLANC

Dry white vermouth, white wine, or Champagne	½ cup (240 ml)
Cold salted butter	14 tablespoons (200 g)
Whitefish or trout roe	4 ounces (110 g)
Flaky sea salt	

1. **Prepare the potato cups:** Scrub the potatoes and pat them dry with tea towels. Pierce each potato with a fork.

2. Preheat the oven to 400°F (200°C). Spread the potatoes in a single layer on a large, rimmed baking sheet. Bake until the potatoes are barely tender when pierced with the tip of a small, sharp knife, 30 to 40 minutes. Let the potatoes cool until easy to handle but not completely cold.

recipe continues ▸

3. Using a sharp knife, cut the potatoes in half crosswise, being careful not to rip the potato skin. Using a teaspoon, scoop out most of the potato flesh, leaving about ⅛ inch (3 mm) of potato with the peel. Now, let the potatoes cool completely, allowing their surfaces to dry, about 2 hours.

    If you wish, you can save the potato flesh for another dish that uses mashed or cooked potatoes.

4. **Prepare the Brussels sprouts:** Taking care not to damage them, peel off the biggest, most perfect leaves from each sprout, as close in size as possible to the potato cups. You need about 7 per person. Save the rest of the Brussels sprouts for another use.

5. Bring a pot of water to a boil. While the water heats up, fill a large bowl with ice water. Add the Brussels sprout leaves to the boiling water just until their color turns a shade brighter, about 3 seconds. Drain the leaves in a colander. Add them to the ice water and let them stand until chilled. Drain them again, and spread the leaves on tea towels to dry. The leaves can be stored at room temperature for up to 2 hours.

6. **Fry the potato cups:** Pour enough oil into a medium saucepan to come halfway up the sides and heat it over medium heat until it is shimmering.

    Test the temperature of the oil with the end of a wooden spoon. When the oil is hot enough, bubbles will rise around the handle.

7. When ready to serve, reheat the oven to 200°F (95°C).

8. Line a baking sheet with paper towels and place it near the stove. Add a few potato cups to the hot oil, pushing them under the surface with a slotted spoon so the oil fills the cups and pulls them down into the oil. Fry until the potato skins are golden brown around their perimeters, about 2 minutes. Using the slotted spoon, transfer the skins to the baking sheet to drain. Repeat with the remaining potato cups. Keep the cups warm in the oven.

    Once you get a feeling for how long these will take to cook, you can add more to the pot at a time. Be sure to let the oil get hot again between batches.

9. **When you have fried about half of the potato cups, start the beurre blanc:** Pour the vermouth into a medium saucepan and bring it to a boil over high heat until it has reduced to about ¼ cup (60 ml), about 5 minutes. Reduce the heat to very low.

10. Cut the butter into small cubes. When the wine comes to a bare simmer, reduce the heat to its lowest setting. Whisk in a few butter cubes. Whisk the butter until it has softened but not melted into a liquid. Continue to whisk in more butter, 2 cubes at a time, occasionally removing the pan from the heat to cool it slightly, until all of the butter has been added and the sauce is smooth but a little thinner than the typical sauce. Adding the butter should take less than 3 minutes. Remove from the heat. The sauce will keep warm for about 20 minutes.

    The butter should be heated just enough that it softens without melting. Don't let the pan get too hot or the sauce will curdle and you will have to start over!

11. Just before serving, reheat the sauce if needed, whisking it over very low heat just until barely warm. Stir in the roe and season to taste with salt.

12. Arrange the Brussels sprout leaves and potato skins on individual plates so they form little cups. Pour the sauce into a small pitcher. At the table, drizzle a few tablespoons of the sauce over the leaves and potatoes, making sure that some of the sauce pools inside each one. Serve with a fork and spoon and pass any remaining sauce on the side.

CONGRATULATIONS: YOU CAN MAKE BEURRE BLANC

This French classic is one of the most basic, but delicious and useful, sauces to know. Just remember to work quickly, moving the saucepan on and off the heat so the butter softens into a creamy mass. Here are just a few ideas for this indispensable beauty of a sauce:

• Add minced fresh dill for a delicate fish sauce.
• Serve with hot or cold steamed asparagus.
• To make a béarnaise sauce to serve with steak, add ½ minced small shallot, 2 teaspoons minced fresh tarragon, and a little freshly ground pepper to the vermouth. Strain out the shallots before serving if you want a smoother sauce, though this is not essential.
• Make "Seal the Deal" pasta on page 111.

MASHED POTATOES AND GREENS WITH SALT-CURED EGG YOLK

SERVES 4

Not every special-occasion dish requires a trip to the gourmet foods store. You really can make this at a moment's notice with ingredients you probably have on hand right now, which is a high-low approach to food that I really enjoy. The first time I made this I was just looking for a way to use up the cooked potato I had left over from making fried potato skins (page 39). I thought about the way the Italians toss a raw egg with hot pasta in truffle season and then shower the dish with shaved truffle for a super-rich, elegant dish. When I added the fresh element of the herbs and greens, it all came together for a starter that looks and feels very restaurant-y. It takes a few steps, but none of them are difficult. If you have a fresh truffle, by all means shave a bit on this as well, but even without it this is a showstopper.

Yukon Gold potatoes	1¼ pounds (600 g)
Large eggs	4
Fine sea salt	2 tablespoons
Salted butter	½ cup (1 stick) (120 g)
Whole milk	¼ cup (40 ml)
Spinach	6 ounces (170 g)
Fresh flat-leaf parsley leaves	30 sprigs
Dill	30 sprigs
Extra-virgin olive oil	3 tablespoons
Fresh bread crumbs	½ cup
Potato chips	½ cup (40 g) coarsely crushed

1. Preheat the oven to 350°F (180°C).

2. Spread the potatoes on a large, rimmed baking sheet. Bake until you can easily pierce them with a knife, about 1 hour. Set aside to cool.

recipe continues ▶

3. While the potatoes are baking, cure the egg yolks. One at a time, separate the eggs, working over a small bowl to catch the whites and carefully slipping each yolk from its shell half into a second small bowl. (You may want to add a couple of extra yolks as insurance against breakage later.)

   When you separate the eggs, hold them close to the bowl. The greater the distance the egg yolk falls, the more likely it is that the yolk will break.

4. Bring 6 cups (1.4 L) water to a boil in a medium saucepan. Add the 2 tablespoons salt and simmer until the salt has dissolved. Pour the hot water into a deep heatproof bowl. Immediately slide the egg yolks into the salted water, holding the bowl as close to the surface of the salt bath as possible to minimize breakage. Let the yolks stand in the water while you prepare the remaining ingredients.

5. When the potatoes are cool enough to handle, cut them in half and scoop the flesh into a medium bowl. Mash the potatoes very well with a potato masher or fork. Set a sieve over a mixing bowl. A few tablespoons at a time, use a rubber spatula to press the potatoes through the sieve, scraping the bottom of the sieve now and then.

   Sieving the potatoes gives them a very fine, silky texture. Don't use a food processor, as the potatoes will become gummy, not light and fluffy.

6. Melt the butter in a small saucepan over low heat. Put the mashed potatoes in a second saucepan over low heat. A few tablespoonfuls at a time, whisk in the melted butter, followed by the milk. Season with salt. Remove from the heat and let stand at room temperature until ready to serve, up to 2 hours.

   The mash will be quite heavy and at times may look like it can't absorb any more butter, but it can, so keep going until it tastes like the richest, nuttiest, silkiest mash you have ever had.

7. Bring a small saucepan of water to a boil over medium-high heat. Discard any tough stems from the spinach. Wash it well.

   Spinach can be very sandy, so to get off any grit, swish it in a sinkful of water, then lift the leaves out into a colander to drain.

8. Coarsely chop the spinach, parsley, and dill. Add to the boiling water and cook just until the spinach and herbs turn a darker shade of green, about 30 seconds. Drain in a sieve and rinse under cold running water, then spread on a tea towel or paper towels to drain and cool.

9. Reheat the potatoes in their pot over very low heat, whisking often to keep them from scorching. While they slowly heat, put the greens in a bowl, drizzle with olive oil, and toss to coat.

10. Heat a pan over medium heat. Add 1 tablespoon of olive oil to the pan, then add the bread crumbs and fry until golden brown. Use a slotted spoon to transfer the bread crumbs onto a paper towel–lined plate.

11. Divide the dressed greens among 4 soup bowls. Top with equal amounts of the potato mash. Use the back of a spoon to make an indentation in each mound of mash. Cupping your fingers, carefully remove one yolk at a time from the salted water, letting the water drip through your fingers, and nestle the yolk in the mash. Sprinkle with the crushed potato chips and bread crumbs. Serve immediately.

SWEET POTATO TOTS
WITH CUMIN BEETS AND SALTED YOGURT

SERVES 6 TO 8

When I traveled to Mumbai, I couldn't stop eating all the wonderful breads, many of which are made with chickpea flour, also known as gram flour. When I returned home, I started experimenting with other ways to use this earthy, toasty gluten-free flour. Since I nearly always have a few roasted sweet potatoes in the refrigerator, and I was still in an Indian state of mind, I came up with these bright orange patties spiked with scallions and spices. Topped with a bit of creamy yogurt and bright red beets, they make a gorgeous finger food. I like them just as well made a bit bigger and topped with an egg (of course) for breakfast. They could also be a vegetarian entrée if you added a vegetable relish or dal, as they would in India.

Sweet potatoes	3 medium, about 1¼ pounds (570 g) total

CUMIN BEETS

Beet	1 large (about 7 ounces/200 g)
Cumin seeds	2 teaspoons
Lemon	½
Extra-virgin olive oil	2 tablespoons

SALTED YOGURT

Plain whole-milk yogurt	1 cup (240 ml)
Fine sea salt	¾ teaspoon

Shallot	1 small
Scallions	2, white and light green parts
Garlic cloves	3
Fresh ginger	1 (2-inch/5-cm) piece
Ground turmeric	1 teaspoon
Sweet paprika	1 teaspoon
Garbanzo bean (chickpea) flour	3 cups (285 g), as needed
Fine sea salt	
Canola oil	⅓ cup (75 ml), as needed

recipe continues ▸

1. Preheat the oven to 400°F (200°F).

2. **Bake the sweet potatoes:** Scrub the potatoes under cold running water but leave them unpeeled. Pierce each a few times with a fork. Place on a large, rimmed baking sheet. Bake until they are tender when pierced with the tip of a small knife, about 1 hour. Let them cool completely.

   If you happen to have roasted sweet potatoes in the fridge, you can skip this step.

3. **Make the cumin beets:** Peel the beet. Grate it on the large holes of a box grater into a large bowl. Use a mortar and pestle to crush the cumin seeds or crush them on a chopping board with a heavy saucepan. Add to the beet. Squeeze in the lemon juice, drizzle with the oil, and toss well. Let stand at room temperature until ready to serve.

4. **Make the salted yogurt:** Mix the yogurt and salt in a small serving bowl, cover, and refrigerate.

5. Line a large, rimmed baking sheet with parchment paper. Scoop the flesh out of the sweet potatoes into a medium bowl. Peel the shallot. Finely chop the shallot and scallions and add to the sweet potatoes. Crush the garlic cloves with the flat side of your knife and discard the papery skins. Use the tip of a teaspoon to scrape the skin from the gingerroot. Using a Microplane or the small holes of a box grater, grate the ginger and garlic into the sweet potato mixture. Add the turmeric and paprika and mix well. Adding one cup at a time, mix in the garbanzo bean flour. Season with salt. Shape the mixture into patties about 2½ inches (6 cm) wide and ½ inch (12 mm) thick. Transfer the patties to the prepared baking sheet.

   If the dough sticks to your hands, mix in a bit more garbanzo bean flour.

6. Heat the oil in a large skillet over medium-low heat until the oil is shimmering but not smoking. Add 2 or 3 patties to the pan and cook until there are golden brown patches on the undersides, about 2 minutes. Flip the patties and cook until the other side looks the same, about 2 minutes more. Transfer the patties to a large serving platter. Cook the remaining patties in batches, adding more oil to the skillet as needed.

7. Add the beet and yogurt bowls to the platter and place it on the counter so your guests can help themselves to the patties and top them with a bit of yogurt and a spoonful of beets.

GREEN ASPARAGUS WITH POACHED EGG

SERVES 4

Making poached eggs was always frustrating until I learned this technique from the great Juan Mari Arzak, of the wonderful restaurant in San Sebastián, Spain. Unlike the conventional method of cooking them in an open pan of water, where I always seemed to end up with half the white floating on the surface of the pan, this method preserves all of the white and always guarantees perfect, unbroken yolks. Now, I can poach ten eggs at once and they will all be just right. Eggs and asparagus go together naturally, but serving them like a green version of "eggs and soldiers" so the spears can be dipped in the soft yolk is a playful presentation. If you can buy goat's milk butter, it is delicious in place of regular butter, with an assertive, almost cheesy flavor that really enhances the spring freshness of the asparagus. For breakfast, you could use fried eggs instead of poached, or you could serve the asparagus as a side dish without the eggs. You'll need kitchen twine for this recipe.

Large eggs	4
Olive oil	2 teaspoons, as needed
Asparagus	16 spears
Canola oil	1 tablespoon
Salted butter	2 tablespoons
Fine sea salt	
Freshly ground black pepper	

1. Line a small bowl or cup with a 10-inch (25-cm) piece of plastic wrap, pressing it down into the bowl and letting the excess hang over the sides. Generously oil the part in the bowl with your fingers or coat it with oil from a spray bottle.

   Watch that the cutting blade does not make small holes in the plastic wrap when you tear it off the roll, or the egg will leak out.

2. Carefully crack one egg into the lined bowl. Gather up the plastic wrap and twist until you've created a small pouch. Tightly tie the pouch closed with

recipe continues ▸

CONGRATULATIONS: YOU CAN MAKE PERFECT POACHED EGGS

Usually, when people say "put an egg on it" they mean a fried egg, but sometimes the cleaner, softer flavor of a poached egg fits the bill even better. Here are some ways to serve them:

• Drop one into your serving of vegetable soup or ramen.
• Top your morning porridge with one.
• Add one to a bowl of freshly cooked greens like spinach or kale.
• Serve one on top of a slice of toasted crusty bread, along with some avocado slices or crisp bacon.

kitchen twine, knotting it as close to the egg as possible. Repeat with the remaining eggs.

Try to press out any air in the pouch as you knot it. The more times you try this, the easier and faster it gets!

3. Bring a pot of water to a boil. While the water heats up, start preparing the asparagus. Trim off the woody ends of the spears. Lightly peel the rest of the asparagus with a vegetable peeler.

   Make sure to clean the asparagus tips well because often there is still some sand in them.

4. The water in the pot should be boiling by now. Carefully drop the egg pouches into the boiling water, making sure the twine doesn't hang over the edge of the pot. Reduce the heat to medium and set a timer for 4 minutes. When the timer goes off, check the eggs: the whites should be just set and opaque. Move the pot to the sink and run cold water into the pot until the water is cool enough to fish out the egg bundles and move them to a plate.

   If you prefer your eggs a bit more set, cook them for 5 minutes.

5. Heat a skillet large enough to hold the asparagus in a single layer over medium-high heat. Add the oil and heat until the oil is hot but not smoking. Add the asparagus spears and cook without moving them or shaking the pan until they are light brown on the undersides, about 1 minute. Add the butter and let it melt. Now you can give the pan a little shake to turn the asparagus. Using a long-handled spoon, baste the asparagus with the butter for another minute. Transfer the asparagus to a platter.

   Be careful not to overcook the asparagus; you want them to have a lot of crunch.

6. Pat the egg pouches dry and put each one in a small serving bowl. Arrange them on the platter with the asparagus. Serve immediately with salt and pepper for seasoning and scissors for releasing the eggs into the serving dishes. To eat, dip the asparagus into the egg yolks, then use a spoon to scoop up the remaining egg.

ARTICHOKES WITH HERB DIP

SERVES 4 TO 6

Most of the time, artichokes are served one per guest, but I think it is much more fun to put them in the center of the island and let everyone share. There is something very satisfying about bringing each leaf to your mouth and scraping off the flesh with your teeth. Eating one leaf at a time keeps your guests occupied while you are busy, and whoever reaches the heart first can trim off any bits of choke, cut it up, and pass it around. In the French countryside, where I spent my summers as a girl, we ate these with just melted butter or classic vinaigrette, but this super herb-packed mayo makes them even better, and gives them an almost meaty quality. All three of my kids love this dish, both for the flavor and the entertainment.

Large artichokes	3

HERB DIP

Large egg yolk	1, at room temperature
Fresh lemon juice	1 teaspoon
Dijon mustard	½ teaspoon
Grainy Dijon mustard	½ teaspoon
Canola or grapeseed oil	¾ cup (180 ml)
Shallot	1 small
Cornichons, drained	12 (50 g)
Capers, drained	2 tablespoons
Fresh chives	20
Fresh sage leaves	20
Fresh tarragon leaves	20
Fresh cilantro leaves	20
Fresh dill sprigs	20
Fresh flat-leaf parsley sprigs	20
Sour cream	½ cup (120 ml)
Fine sea salt	

recipe continues ▸

1. **Cook the artichokes:** Place the artichokes, stem ends up, in a large pot of water. Cover and bring to a boil over high heat. Reduce the heat to medium and boil for 45 minutes to 1 hour. Do not overcook.

   The boiling time will depend on the size of the artichoke, so cook them just until an outer leaf comes off with just a little resistance.

2. Drain the artichokes in a large colander and turn them upside down so that all the remaining water can run out. Let cool.

3. Whisk the egg yolk, lemon juice, Dijon mustard, and grainy mustard in a medium bowl until combined. Drizzle in the oil about 1 teaspoon at a time, whisking until you have a nice thick mayo. This should take a couple of minutes, so don't rush it.

   The flavor of the dip will not be as good with store-bought mayonnaise!

4. Finely chop the shallot, cornichons, capers, chives, sage, and tarragon and add to the mayonnaise. Finely chop the cilantro leaves, dill, and parsley sprigs (you can include a little of the thin stems) and stir them in. Add the sour cream and fold the mixture together. Season to taste with the salt. Taste the dip with a piece of flatbread to check for seasoning.

   If the dip needs more acidity, add more lemon juice, cornichons, or capers. Add more herbs if you like, too.

5. Cut each artichoke vertically in half. Use a dessert spoon to scoop out and discard the hairy choke. Arrange the artichokes on a large platter with the bowl of dip, and set out a bowl for the used leaves. Let the guests peel off leaves and dunk them into the herb dip.

You are likely to have leftover dip from this starter. It can be covered and refrigerated for about 5 days. Use the leftover herb sauce (or the Porcini Mayo on page 59) to:

• Toss with hot boiled potatoes to give them a tasty glaze.
• Spread on sandwiches, especially fried fish sandwiches.
• Serve as a dip for the homemade potato chips on page 29.
• Substitute for plain mayonnaise in egg salad.

QUAIL EGGS WITH PORCINI MAYONNAISE

SERVES 4 TO 6

Before he opened Noma, René was a sous-chef at another local restaurant, near our home, with a very traditional French menu. We often went there on our days off. We could have had anything on the menu, but what I liked best was sitting in the lounge, where boiled quail eggs served with a porcini purée was their idea of a bar snack. Earthy dried porcini mushrooms aren't quite as over-the-top luxurious as truffles, but I find everyone enjoys peeling, dipping, and popping these perfect little mouthfuls. If you can't get quail eggs, you can use quartered hard-boiled eggs; it just won't be quite as much fun to eat. If you wish, add 1 teaspoon of minced fresh chives to the mayonnaise.

PORCINI MAYONNAISE

Dried porcini	1 ounce (27 g)
Salted butter	1 teaspoon
Garlic clove	1 small
Grapeseed or canola oil	¾ cup (180 ml)
Large egg yolk	1, at room temperature
Fresh lemon juice	½ teaspoon
Dijon mustard	½ teaspoon
Fine sea salt	
Freshly ground black pepper	
Fresh chives	½ teaspoon finely chopped (optional)
Fresh flat-leaf parsley	½ teaspoon finely chopped (optional)
Quail eggs	2 dozen at room temperature
Fine sea salt	1 teaspoon

1. **Make the mayonnaise:** Place the dried porcini in a small bowl and add boiling water to cover. Let the mushrooms stand until softened, about 30 minutes. Drain the mushrooms in a sieve and rinse them well twice to remove all of the grit. Spread them on tea towels or paper towels to drain then pat dry.

recipe continues ▸

2. Melt the butter in a medium saucepan over medium heat. Crush the garlic clove with the flat side of your knife and discard the papery skin. Add the drained mushrooms and the garlic to the butter. Cook, stirring occasionally, for 3 to 5 minutes, until the liquid evaporates. Pour the oil over the mushrooms and turn the heat off. Let the oil cool to room temperature, at least 1 hour.

3. Use a slotted spoon to remove the mushrooms and garlic. Discard the garlic from the oil. Finely chop the porcini. Whisk the egg yolk, lemon juice, and Dijon mustard in a medium bowl until combined. Drizzle in the mushroom oil about 1 tablespoon at a time, whisking until you have a nice thick mayo. This should take a couple of minutes, so don't rush it. Gently stir in the mushrooms. If you want to add the chopped chives or parsley, you can fold them in now.

    Taste the mayo and see if you want to add more lemon juice or mustard to freshen it up, or add a bit more salt and some pepper.

4. Fill a large bowl with ice and water. Place the quail eggs in a medium saucepan with 2 inches of water to cover and bring them to a gentle boil over moderately high heat. Take them off the heat, cover the eggs, and let stand for 5 minutes, then drain them and place them in the ice water to cool.

    Use a timer to be sure you don't overcook the eggs.

5. Put the quail eggs and porcini mayonnaise in separate serving bowls. Let your guests peel the eggs and dip them into the mayo. Leftover mayonnaise can be covered and refrigerated for up to 3 days.

CONGRATULATIONS: YOU CAN MAKE HOMEMADE MAYONNAISE

You probably already know mayo is amazing with so many things but you probably didn't know how simple it is to make, even without a blender or food processor (although if you prefer to use either one, it's even faster to make). Flavor it with curry powder, a single herb such as tarragon or chives, chile sauce or sriracha, more citrus—really, anything you like. You can also substitute this for the herb sauce when serving boiled artichokes.

WHITE ASPARAGUS
WITH TRUFFLE SAUCE

SERVES 4

This is probably the most sophisticated finger food you'll ever see. White asparagus, which is covered with soil as it grows to keep the spears from producing the chlorophyll that turns them green, is far more common in Europe than it is in the United States and also generally more expensive. But for an occasional splurge it's worth trying, especially for a high-impact dish like this one. It was inspired by a very elegant starter I had as part of a multicourse meal at Alain Ducasse's restaurant Le Louis XV in Monaco. He served different marinated crudités with a purée of decadent fresh truffles, and it was the course that really lingered in my memory. My version uses preserved truffles, so it's a little gentler on the budget but still very impressive. Winter truffles have more flavor than summer truffles, but you could use either. I prefer this as a finger food, but you could also plate the spears and serve them with a small spoonful of the truffle sauce.

TRUFFLE SAUCE

Salted butter	½ cup (110 g)
Preserved black truffles	1 (2.8-ounce/90-g) jar, whole or sliced
Large egg yolks	3, at room temperature
Veal or duck demi-glace	1 tablespoon (optional)
Flaky sea salt	

White asparagus	16 spears
Grapeseed or canola oil	2 teaspoons
Salted butter	1 tablespoon
Flaky sea salt	

1. **Make the truffle sauce:** Melt the butter in a small saucepan over low heat. Remove from the heat and let it cool to tepid—you should be able to stick your finger in it comfortably.

recipe continues ▸

2. Drain the truffles if packed in oil and shave off a few slices to use for garnish if they are whole. Place the rest of the truffles in a food processor and purée until smooth. Add the egg yolks and process until combined. With the machine running, add the melted butter—the mixture will thicken quickly. Add the demi-glace. Season to taste with salt. Transfer the sauce to a small serving bowl and set aside for 20 to 30 minutes.

   If your truffles are packed in water, add the liquid to the puree; it has a lot of flavor.

3. **Cook the asparagus:** Make sure to clean the asparagus tips well because they can retain sand. Trim off the woody ends, which are tough and bitter. Lightly peel the stems with a vegetable peeler.

   Cut rather than break off the ends of the spears; I find breaking them removes more stem than necessary.

4. Heat a skillet large enough to hold the asparagus in a single layer over medium-high heat. Add the oil, followed by the asparagus. Do not shake the pan—just let the asparagus cook without moving until they are lightly browned on the underside, about 2 minutes. Add the butter and let it melt. Now you can give the pan a little shake to turn the asparagus. Use a long-handled spoon to spoon the butter over the asparagus and cook for another 30 seconds or so.

   You are just cooking the spears to get them hot, not tender. They should stay very crunchy.

5. Transfer the asparagus to a platter and sprinkle with salt. Serve with the truffle sauce for dipping.

BUTTER-FRIED BREAD
WITH TOMATOES

SERVES 6

Go simple bruschetta one better by doubling down on the tomato flavor and crisping the bread in butter rather than just toasting it. It seems like a lot of butter—and it is—but it tastes so good, so don't be skimpy. You can use any mixture of cherry, heirloom, or yellow tomatoes you find at the market, as long as the amount is about the same as five good-sized tomatoes. Day-old bread is just fine for this, and in fact it's a great way to use up those odds and ends. If you have fresh basil, 10 to 12 leaves, is a nice addition.

Large, ripe tomatoes	5
Fine sea salt	
Crusty bread, such as ciabatta	6 (½-inch/12-mm) slices
Salted butter	12 tablespoons (170 g), as needed
Extra-virgin olive oil	3 tablespoons
Freshly ground black pepper	
Fresh basil leaves	12 large (optional)

1. To core the tomatoes easily, slice downward next to but not through the stem. Make two angled cuts into the larger half to release the core and discard. Cut the tomatoes into small dice.

2. Put the chopped tomatoes in a sieve placed over a bowl to catch their juices and sprinkle with about ½ teaspoon salt. Leave the tomatoes to drain for at least 30 minutes, stirring them gently every 10 or 15 minutes.

   If you have the time, drain the tomatoes for a full hour; the more liquid they give off, the more concentrated their flavor will be.

3. Cut the biggest bread slices into two or three pieces.

4. Put a large skillet over low to medium heat and add 3 tablespoons of the butter. When the butter has melted and starts bubbling a little, add a few

recipe continues ▸

slices of bread. Fry until the bread is golden brown, about 1½ minutes. Add 1 tablespoon more butter to the pan and, when it's melted, turn the bread and brown on the second side for another 1½ minutes. Drain the fried bread on paper towels in a single layer; don't pile them up, as they will lose their crispness. Fry the remaining bread slices, adding more butter to the pan as needed.

5. With a slotted spoon, transfer the drained tomatoes to a bowl, reserving the juices for another use (see sidebar). Drizzle the tomatoes with the olive oil, add the pepper, and stir gently. Add salt to taste if needed.

   Because the tomatoes have already been salted, you may not need any additional salt at this point.

6. Arrange the bread on a plate and top with the tomatoes. Serve right away so that the toasts don't become soggy.

TOMATO WATER

The juices that drain off of salted tomatoes are full of flavor and can be used in many ways:

• Add it to any vegetable soup.
• Mix it into your favorite tomato sauces to boost the tomato flavor (see pages 111–128).
• Whisk it into a vinaigrette.

This recipe will also yield enough tomato water for one perfect Bloody Mary: Pour 1 fluid ounce (2 tablespoons/30 ml) of your favorite vodka into an ice-filled glass. Fill the glass halfway with the tomato water (it will only be a few tablespoons) and top it off with a good tonic water, such as Fever-Tree. Stir with a celery or cucumber stick and enjoy.

TURMERIC-FRIED BREAD
WITH HERBED EGGPLANT

SERVES 6

René and I are so lucky to have my mother living with us; she helps out in more ways than I can count! She would be the first to admit, however, that kitchen cleanup is not her strong suit, which is how this dish came to be. I was frying some bread in a pan I thought had been cleaned (it was back in the cupboard), and I realized the toasts were picking up the yellow color of turmeric from the last dish that had been cooked in it. Fortunately, I loved both the look and the flavor, so all's well that ends well. This is a great example of how you can take a base recipe like Butter-Fried Bread with Tomatoes (page 65) and pump up the flavor by layering additional seasonings onto the individual components. For the topping, instead of simple, uncooked tomatoes, I've paired the bread with a savory eggplant mash that benefits from lots and lots of chopped fresh herbs. If you grow lovage in your garden as so many of us in Denmark do, you'll find that its subtle cucumber flavor is fantastic with the eggplant, but use whatever tender green herbs you can get readily.

EGGPLANT AND HERBS

Eggplants	2 large, about 3 pounds (1.4 kg)
Fine sea salt	
Extra-virgin olive oil	1¼ cups (300 ml), as needed
Fresh cilantro sprigs	20
Fresh dill sprigs	20
Fresh flat-leaf parsley sprigs	20
Fresh lovage leaves	20 large (optional)
Freshly ground black pepper	

TURMERIC-FRIED BREAD

Crusty rustic bread, such as ciabatta	6 (½-inch/12-mm) slices
Salted butter	4 tablespoons (55 g)
Ground turmeric	½ teaspoon

recipe continues ▸

1. **Prepare the eggplants:** Cut the eggplants into ¾-inch (2-cm) dice. Put in a colander and toss with about ½ teaspoon salt. Let drain for 30 to 60 minutes. Rinse well, drain briefly, and spread onto tea towels to pat dry.

2. Heat ½ cup (115 ml) of the oil in a deep pot over moderately high heat until the oil is hot but not smoking. Add a quarter of the eggplant to the pot and cook until golden brown on the bottom, about 2 minutes. Push the browned eggplant to one side of the skillet. Add another ¼ cup of oil to the pan and when it's hot, add another quarter of the cubed eggplant. Continue cutting and cooking the eggplant, letting each batch brown for 2 minutes and adding more oil as needed.

3. Cover the pot with the lid askew. Reduce the heat to low and cook, stirring occasionally, until the eggplant is a tender, chunky mash, about 15 minutes.

4. Coarsely chop the cilantro, dill, parsley, and lovage leaves, if using. (You can include some of the tender stems near the leaves.) Reserve 2 tablespoons of the chopped herbs for garnish and stir the remaining herbs into the eggplant. Season to taste with salt and pepper. Remove from the heat.

5. **Make the fried bread:** Line a baking sheet with paper towels. Cut the biggest bread slices into two or three pieces. Line up a double thickness of paper towels on the counter near the stove. Melt 4 tablespoons of the butter in a large skillet over medium heat. When the butter starts bubbling, stir in the turmeric. Add the bread and fry until the underside is golden brown, about 1½ minutes. Turn the bread and brown on the second side for another 1½ minutes. Drain on paper towels in a single layer; don't stack them, or they will lose their crispness.

   Don't be misled by the turmeric, which will turn the bread slices golden yellow; keep cooking until they are a nicely toasted brown.

6. Pile the bread slices on a plate. Mound the eggplant in a serving bowl and sprinkle with the reserved herbs.

CHICKEN LIVERS AND AVOCADO
ON RYE BREAD

SERVES 4

It's fun to take something familiar from childhood and reinvent it as a sophisticated, grown-up appetizer. Dark sourdough rye bread topped with a thick slice of leverpastete—a cross between pâté and American liverwurst—is standard lunch-box fare for every Danish child. I've deconstructed that combination into a dish that's a little lighter and a lot easier to make, without all the puréeing and molding. Danish guests always smile when they try this dressed-up version of a familiar old friend, but even if you didn't grow up eating chicken livers, give this savory combination a try. Look for a good, chewy whole-kernel sourdough rye bread; otherwise, use any dense whole-grain bread. These can be eaten with a fork and knife or as a crostini.

Salted butter	2 tablespoons, at room temperature
Dark rye bread	4 slices
Chicken livers	12 ounces (340 g)
Salted butter	2 tablespoons, at room temperature
Canola oil	3 tablespoons
Veal demiglace	¼ cup (120 ml)
Flaky sea salt	
Avocado	1
Fresh chives	25
Lemon	1
Freshly ground black pepper	To taste

1. Preheat the oven to 350°F (180°C)

2. Butter the bread on both sides and arrange the slices on a large, rimmed baking sheet. Bake, turning the bread over halfway during baking, until the bread is a bit darker around the edges, 8 to 10 minutes. Transfer to a wire rack to cool.

recipe continues ▸

3. While the bread toasts, drain the chicken livers and pat them as dry as possible with paper towels. Trim the livers and cut them into large, bite-sized pieces.

    Handling raw livers takes some getting used to—hang in there! You may find small globs of fat or veins attached; just trim them off with a small sharp knife.

4. Heat the oil in a large skillet over medium-high heat until it is shimmering but not smoking. Add the livers in a single layer. Cook without moving them until they are caramel brown on the bottom, about 2 minutes. Flip the livers and brown the other side, about 2 minutes more.

    Don't crowd the chicken livers in the center of the pan, or they won't brown properly and will give off too much liquid.

5. Add the broth and bring to a boil. Tilt the skillet so the broth pools on one side. Use a long-handled spoon to baste the livers a few times to give them a glaze, about 1 minute. Cut into a liver to be sure it is done—it should be pink, not red. Simmer 1 minute longer, if necessary. Season with salt and remove from the heat.

6. Cut the avocado in half lengthwise. Twist the halves to separate them. Hold the half with the pit in one hand. Holding the knife in your other hand, rap the knife blade into the pit to lodge it there. Twist the knife to loosen and remove the pit. Use the tip of the knife to cut the avocado flesh lengthwise into thin slices. Use a large spoon to scoop out the flesh onto a plate. Repeat with the other half.

7. To assemble the toasts, thinly slice the chives. Cut the rye toasts in half and arrange on a serving platter. Top with equal amounts of the avocado slices, followed by the chicken livers (cut the larger ones in half, as needed). Drizzle with the pan juices. Squeeze a little lemon juice over all. Season the toasts with pepper and flaky salt, sprinkle with the chives, and serve immediately.

DEMIGLACE

I am lucky to be able to buy demiglace—veal, chicken, beef—from my butcher. It comes in a jellied state and I divide leftovers into 2-tablespoon portions and freeze them. They are so handy to have for enriching sauces, and in a pinch you can add them to water to make stock. If you aren't as fortunate, demiglace is available in most gourmet food shops in a shelf-stable package or jar. It is also fairly easy to make your own by cooking down unsalted stock until it is about one tenth its original volume.

DEEP-FRIED EGGPLANT
WITH RICOTTA AND SAGE

SERVES 4

When I was rooting through the fridge for a snack one day, I found a few pieces of battered and fried eggplant left over from making the Eggplant Gratin on page 108. I topped them with creamy ricotta and crackly fried fresh sage leaves and I liked it so much I now make these all the time. The eggplant has a deliciously rich, salty flavor, and the two-stage frying process makes it extra crisp. This could easily become a light lunch or dinner if you leave the slices whole and top the cheese with a few slices of tomato and Ibérico ham, or even use two pieces of eggplant to make a sandwich.

Eggplant	1 medium
Fine sea salt	1 teaspoon, plus more for sprinkling
Canola oil, for deep-frying	1 quart (960 ml), as needed
Fresh sage leaves	30 large
Unbleached all-purpose flour	1 cup (140 g)
Large eggs	3
Pecorino romano or Parmigiano-Reggiano cheese	2 cups (250 g) freshly grated
Ricotta cheese	1 cup (250 g)
Extra-virgin olive oil	For drizzling

1. Cut the eggplant lengthwise into slices about ¼ inch (6 mm) thick. Lightly sprinkle on both sides with the 1 teaspoon salt *(this will help draw out the liquid)* and lay the slices on tea towels. Let stand for about 30 minutes. Wipe dry with the towels.

2. Pour enough oil into a large, heavy saucepan to come halfway up the sides and place over medium heat until the oil is shimmering.

   Test the temperature of the oil with the end of a wooden spoon. When the oil is hot enough, bubbles will rise around the handle.

recipe continues ▸

3. Line a plate with paper towels. A few at a time, add the sage leaves to the oil and fry until they are the shade of dark autumn leaves and a little transparent, just a few seconds. Immediately use a slotted spoon to transfer the sage to the paper towels to drain and cool.

   Don't pile the leaves on top of each other, as that will cause them to lose their crispness.

4. Line a baking sheet with paper towels near the stove. In batches, carefully add 2 slices of the eggplant to the hot oil, using tongs to keep the slices fully submerged. Deep-fry until they are golden brown, about 2 minutes. Using a wire skimmer, transfer the eggplant to the paper towels. Let the eggplant cool at least 5 minutes. Turn the temperature under the oil to low but don't turn it off.

   You are just partially cooking the eggplant at this point; without this step it might not cook all the way through when it is breaded and fried.

5. Put the flour in a wide, shallow bowl. Whisk the eggs in a second shallow bowl until well blended, then whisk in the grated cheese.

6. When you are ready to bread and fry the eggplant, reheat the oil until shimmering again (retest with your wooden spoon). Working near the stove, line up the eggplant, the bowl of flour, and the egg mixture. Have a baking sheet or platter lined with fresh paper towels nearby. One at a time, coat the eggplant slices evenly in the flour, then in the egg and cheese mixture, and carefully slide them into the hot oil. Fry the eggplant, turning once, until golden brown, about 2 minutes. Use a slotted spatula or your tongs to transfer the eggplant to the paper towels.

   Once you have done the first couple of slices, you might feel comfortable cooking 2 to 4 slices at a time, but do not crowd the pot or they won't fry properly.

7. Top the warm eggplant slices with the ricotta, fried sage, a drizzle of olive oil, and a sprinkle of salt. Cut each slice into 2 or 3 pieces, arrange them on a platter, and serve hot.

BREADED TOMATOES
WITH MASCARPONE AND SARDINES

SERVES 4

You'll find tinned fish in virtually every Scandinavian pantry, and it's just the thing for pulling together spur-of-the-moment snacks like this easy starter. The ingredients are the kind I usually have on hand, though if I didn't have mascarpone, it would be easy to substitute another creamy, mild cheese, like ricotta or even a bit of Greek yogurt. Pick a meaty tomato such as beefsteak or an heirloom variety. It's fine if they're a bit underripe; you want them firm enough to hold up to frying. My middle daughter isn't a fan of sardines, so for her I wrap the breaded tomato in a slice of mortadella, like a deconstructed sandwich, which is pretty good as well! I usually eat and serve this as a finger food in the kitchen or at the table with a glass of wine, but you could serve it with cutlery if you want to be a bit more formal.

Large, firm-ripe tomatoes	2
Unbleached all-purpose flour	1 cup (140 g)
Large eggs	2
Panko bread crumbs	1 cup (65 g)
Canola oil, for frying	2 cups (480 ml), as needed
Mascarpone	1 cup (225 ml)
Flaky sea salt	
Sardines in olive oil	2 (3.75-ounce/105-g) cans

1. Slice the tomatoes about ⅓ inch (8 mm) thick. Put the flour in a wide, shallow bowl. Crack the eggs into a second shallow bowl and beat them well with a fork. Put the panko in a third shallow bowl.

2. Heat a large skillet over medium heat. Add enough oil to come ⅓ inch (8 mm) up the sides of the pan and heat until the oil is shimmering.

3. While the oil heats, dip a tomato slice in the flour and turn to coat evenly. Next, dip it in the eggs, allowing the excess to drip back into the bowl, then

recipe continues ▸

dredge it in the panko. Set it on a plate and repeat with the remaining tomato slices.

Remember to keep an eye on the oil while you're breading the tomatoes; you don't want it to start smoking! If it does, remove it from the heat for a minute before you begin to fry.

4. Set a wire rack on a rimmed baking sheet. One at a time, carefully add a few of the breaded tomato slices to the hot oil. After a minute or so, use silicone-tipped tongs or a metal spatula to carefully peek at the bottoms of the tomatoes. If they are golden brown, turn them and cook the second side until golden brown, about 1 minute more. Transfer the tomatoes to the wire rack or a paper towel–lined plate to drain while you fry the remaining tomato slices. Once you have fried all the slices, let them cool for 5 to 10 minutes.

Don't overcrowd the pan, or the slices won't fry up nice and crisp.

5. Arrange the tomatoes on a big plate in a single layer to preserve their crispness. Stir the mascarpone to loosen it up and spoon a little bit onto each tomato. Top each with a sardine and sprinkle each one with a bit of salt. Serve immediately.

LEEKS WITH VINAIGRETTE, BACON, AND PINE NUTS

SERVES 4

As long as I can remember, my mother has been making a version of this ultra-classical dish, a recipe she picked up as an au pair in Paris. She always served it cold as a salad course, but I prefer it warm as a starter—it's so nice with a glass of Champagne. Basil is not traditional, but the slight licorice flavor works well with the leeks. Once you've made this a few times, you'll see how versatile it is; I think it's substantial enough to be an entrée with a piece of rye toast, especially for a summer evening, or a simple, elegant side if you leave off the bacon and pine nuts.

Leeks	3 large
Salted butter	3 tablespoons
Pine nuts	⅓ cup (20 g)
Grapeseed or canola oil	2 teaspoons
Bacon	10 ounces (280 g)

LEMON VINAIGRETTE

Fresh lemon juice	2 teaspoons
Dijon mustard	1 teaspoon
Extra-virgin olive oil	¼ cup (60 ml), as needed
Fine sea salt	
Freshly ground black pepper	

1. Bring a medium pot of about 1 quart (960 ml) water to a boil over high heat.

2. **Clean the leeks well:** Cut off the root end of the leek and about half of the pale green top. Split the leek lengthwise. Rinse the leeks well under cold running water, making sure to open up the layers and wash away any dirt between the layers while keeping each piece intact.

recipe continues ▶

3. Cut the leeks crosswise into pieces 2 to 3 inches long. When the water is boiling, add the butter and leeks to the water and return to a boil. Reduce the heat to low and cover. Gently simmer the leeks for 15 to 20 minutes, or until they are just tender when pierced with the tip of a sharp knife but they still hold their shape.

4. Heat a small, dry skillet over medium heat. Add the pine nuts to the pan and cook, shaking the pan every 20 to 30 seconds, until they are lightly toasted. Pour the nuts out onto a plate.

   Don't let the pine nuts stand in the skillet, or they will continue to toast and eventually burn.

5. Wipe out the pan. Add the grapeseed oil and heat it over medium heat. Cut the bacon into strips about ¼ inch (6 mm) wide and 2 inches (5 cm) long. Add the bacon to the pan and cook, stirring occasionally, until it is crisp and brown, about 6 minutes. Using a slotted spoon, remove the bacon from the pan and put on paper towels to drain.

6. **Make the vinaigrette:** Whisk the lemon juice and mustard in a small bowl until smooth. Stir in the olive oil a little at a time.

7. Arrange the leeks on a platter. Pour the dressing over the leeks and season them with salt and pepper. Sprinkle them with the bacon and pine nuts and season with more salt and pepper. Serve warm or at room temperature.

CONGRATULATIONS: YOU CAN MAKE A VINAIGRETTE

Everyone should know how to make this simple dressing by heart. Just about every salad dressing is a variation on this fundamental theme of acid-plus-oil flavored with a bit of mustard. The mustard isn't just there for flavor; it also acts as a thickener to give the dressing body. Tweak the proportions to get the balance you like best. Once you have it down, here are some suggestions to get you started:

• Switch up the lemon juice for your favorite vinegar.
• Add finely minced shallots or garlic.
• Drizzle in a touch of maple syrup or honey.
• Mix in tender herbs, such as chives, dill, tarragon, or parsley.

MANILA CLAMS WITH GARLIC AND TOASTED BREAD CRUMBS

SERVES 4

Considering that Denmark is surrounded by water, it's surprising that shellfish isn't more popular here. Having grown up eating pan-roasted clams and mussels both in Portugal and France, where they are found on every bistro menu, I find their briny, chewy taste a great light way to start a meal. Serving them right out of the bowl, as finger food, is a little messy, but it's really the best way to get every bit of those yummy crumbs, which soak up the clam juice and garlic so deliciously. Everyone is always surprised at how quickly this dish comes together—and how good it is.

Manila clams or cockles	2 pounds (910 g)
Crusty bread	6 slices, preferably slightly stale
Extra-virgin olive oil	3 tablespoons
Flaky sea salt	1 teaspoon, or to taste
Garlic cloves	4
Fresh flat-leaf parsley	25 sprigs
Canola oil	3 tablespoons
Red pepper flakes	½ teaspoon, or to taste
Salted butter	1 tablespoon

1. Scrub the clams under cold running water. Soak them in a large bowl of salted water while you prep the other ingredients.

2. Preheat the oven to 350°F (180°C)

3. Tear the bread into a few pieces. Place in a food processor or blender and chop into coarse crumbs. Spread the crumbs on a rimmed baking sheet. Drizzle with the olive oil, season with salt, and toss well with your hands. Bake the crumbs, stirring occasionally with a spatula, until they are golden brown and crisp, 10 to 12 minutes. Set the crumbs aside to cool.

   Check on the bread crumbs and stir them occasionally, because the crumbs near the edges of the pan tend to brown first.

recipe continues ▸

4. Crush the garlic cloves with the flat side of your knife and discard the papery skins. Cut the garlic cloves lengthwise into very thin slices as finely as you can. Coarsely chop the parsley leaves (you can use a little of the tender stems).

5. Drain the clams. If any are open, tap them lightly against the sink. If they close up, they can be cooked. If not, throw them away.

6. Heat the canola oil in a large skillet over medium-high heat. Add the clams, then the garlic and red pepper flakes. Bring to a boil and cook, uncovered, stirring often, for about 4 minutes. Add the butter and cook until it has melted and all of the clams are open, about 1 minute more.

   Clams that do not open when you cook them should be thrown away. Never try to force a clam open if it is closed.

7. Mix the bread crumbs and parsley in a serving bowl. Add the clams and the pan juices and toss quickly to combine. Serve immediately so the crumbs don't become soggy, along with a bowl for the shells.

CONGRATULATIONS: YOU CAN MAKE SEASONED BREAD CRUMBS

I can't think of a better use for stale bread. These crunchy little bits give an instant lift to so many things:

• Flavor them with garlic, fresh herbs, grated lemon zest, or your favorite spice blend for another layer of seasoning in meatballs or breaded foods like the fillets on page 183.
• Sprinkle on yogurt along with nuts and some fruit.
• Add them to a pasta dish at the table instead of grated cheese.
• Use them to give a bit of extra texture to roasted vegetables like the cauliflower on page 205.
• Add a handful to a bowl of soup or a salad as you would croutons.

COLD SHRIMP IN HORSERADISH CREAM

SERVES 4

Boiled shrimp served with mayonnaise is a standby of many Scandinavian tables, but with just a little effort you can make something that looks and tastes so much more interesting. When you cut cauliflower paper-thin, as it is in this elegant starter, your plates will look like a beautiful forest. Fresh horseradish, which infuses the cream with its pungent heat, is only available at certain times of the year. If you can't find it at your market, a bit of wasabi paste stirred into 1 tablespoon of cream, then blended with the remaining cream, would be a different but equally delicious option.

Horseradish	1 (1-inch/2.5-cm) piece
Heavy cream	½ cup (120 ml)
Large (25 to 30 count) shrimp	12
Walnut oil	2 tablespoons, plus more for drizzling
Flaky sea salt	
Cauliflower	2 to 3 large florets

1. Peel the horseradish. Using the small holes on a box grater, grate the horseradish into the cream in a small bowl and drop in the ungrated end, too. Cover and set aside to allow the horseradish to infuse the cream for about 15 minutes. Strain the infused cream through a sieve into a small bowl, pressing hard on the horseradish with the back of a spoon. Discard the horseradish. Cover and refrigerate until ready to use.

   Taste the cream before you strain it—it should have a little bite. If not, let it infuse for a few more minutes.

2. Bring a medium saucepan of water to a boil over high heat. Add the shrimp and cook just until they turn pink around the edges, about 1 minute. Drain well and rinse under cold water. Return to the saucepan, fill it with cold running water, and let the shrimp stand until completely cold, about 10 minutes. Peel and devein the shrimp.

   The shrimp should still be a bit soft, not completely cooked through and opaque.

recipe continues ▸

3. Peel the shrimp by pinching the tail segment and pulling it off. Use your thumbs to pull off the rest of the shell, splitting it along the stomach. Using the tip of a knife, make a shallow cut down the back just slightly off center to reveal the dark vein. Remove the vein with the tip of your knife.

4. Place the shrimp on a plate. Brush them with the walnut oil, season them with salt, and let stand for 5 minutes.

5. Cut each cauliflower floret in half lengthwise. Using a mandoline or a V-slicer and starting with the flat, cut side of the cauliflower, cut thin, perfect slices from each half-floret. Set them aside.

   It's hard but not impossible to slice the cauliflower thinly enough with a knife. You want them delicately paper-thin.

6. Cut the shrimp in half lengthwise and arrange 6 halves in a circle in the bottom of 4 shallow bowls. Brush with more walnut oil and top each shrimp with a thin slice of cauliflower. Spoon equal amounts of the horseradish cream in the centers of the bowls.

JERUSALEM ARTICHOKES AND ALMOND MILK SOUP

SERVES 4 TO 5

I get a weekly CSA box from a local farmer, and it forces me to play with vegetables I might not choose myself. Jerusalem artichokes, also called sunchokes, were one of those things I was never entirely sure what to do with besides throw them in a roasting pan. Then I was served a small cup of a thin and creamy almond broth as a welcome gift from the chef at a local restaurant, and I thought what a light and lovely soup the vegetable would make. Even with just a few ingredients, this soup has so many different nutty tones. Serve it in small portions, as it is deceptively rich.

Jerusalem artichokes	9 ounces (255 g)
Chicken broth	1½ cups (360 ml)
Pine nuts	¼ cup (15 g)
Plain unsweetened almond milk	1¼ cups (300 ml)
Fine sea salt	
Salted butter	2 tablespoons

1. Peel the artichokes and put them in a medium saucepan. Add the broth and bring to a boil over medium-high heat. Reduce the heat to medium. Cook at a steady simmer, uncovered, until the liquid has reduced to about 3 tablespoons and the artichokes are tender when pierced with the tip of a small, sharp knife, about 25 minutes.

   If the liquid hasn't quite reduced to ¼ cup (60 ml), use a slotted spoon to transfer the artichokes to a bowl, and boil the liquid over high heat until it reduces to that amount. Return the artichokes to the saucepan.

2. Heat a small, dry skillet over medium heat. Add the pine nuts and cook, stirring often, until lightly toasted, about 2 minutes. Pour them out onto a plate and let cool.

   Don't leave the pine nuts in the skillet, or they will keep toasting and eventually burn.

recipe continues ▸

3. Add half of the almond milk to the saucepan and purée the mixture with an immersion blender. Add the remaining almond milk and blend again. (Or purée the soup in a stand blender with the lid ajar to vent any steam.) Season with salt. Keep the soup warm over very low heat.

4. For a brown butter garnish, cut the butter into tablespoons. Melt the butter in a medium saucepan over medium heat until it foams. Continue to cook, stirring constantly with a whisk, until the butter smells nutty and the sediment on the bottom of the pan is light brown, about 2 minutes. Remove from the heat.

5. Raise the heat under the soup to medium-high and whisk constantly until it comes to a simmer. Divide the soup among 4 small bowls or mugs, sprinkle with the pine nuts, and drizzle with the brown butter. Serve immediately.

MAINS

If starters generally mean finger food to me, when it comes to mains, I like something you'll need to approach with a fork and knife: savory, satisfying, with lots of bold flavors and textures. Sometimes that means meat—roasted, braised, pan-seared, or even fried—but we have meatless meals several times a week and I've found you can get just as much comforting heft and taste from a vegetable entrée if you approach it as you would another protein.

During a hectic week of juggling homework, diapers, and bedtime stories, using the oven to bake or roast food is so easy and allows me to cook a delicious meal with almost zero effort. Roasting a chicken, cooking a whole fish in a salt crust, or cooking ribs and sweet potatoes gives me a little extra time to have fun with the kids while dinner does its thing unattended (and there is only one baking dish to wash afterward). The best thing about roasting food, though, is the comforting way it slowly fills the house with the most amazing scents and brings everyone to the table. When I'm looking for something really quick, I usually opt for something pan-fried, first of all because it makes food taste absolutely delicious but also because it usually means that dinner will be on the table within thirty minutes. Eggs are probably the most used and versatile ingredients in my kitchen and I love everything about them. If for some reason I don't make it to the store, I know I can always combine eggs with things I have on hand, like oats, rice, or vegetables, to make a quick and satisfying meal. Pasta is another weekday standby and I'm always amazed at how it becomes a completely different dish depending on how you top it—even if you're using just a few ingredients.

EASY BAKE OVEN

Baked Salmon with Thyme and Thin Potatoes (10 mins active; 35 mins total) • *Foolproof and simple. Period.* **page 96**

Salt-Crusted Sea Bass with Green Beans (30 mins active; 50 mins total) • *An impressive presentation that is deceptively straightforward* **page 99**

Baked Cod with Crushed Tomatoes and Green Olives (20 mins active; 25 mins total) • *Add veggies and olives for a sophisticated one-pan entrée* **page 102**

Roasted Ratatouille with Orzo (35 mins active; 80 mins total) • *A prettier, hands-free version of the iconic French sauté* **page 105**

Eggplant Gratin (40 mins active; 120 mins total) *Fried, layered, and then baked, a little more prep pays big dividends* **page 108**

PASTA WITH TOMATO SAUCE, IN SIX ACTS

BIG BOWLS

EGGS FOR DINNER

SWIFT SKILLET DINNERS

Monkfish with Lemon Sauce and Peas
(20 mins active; 20 mins total) • *A nice and easy approach to fish cookery for a busy night* page 165

Flank Steak with Oven-Fried Garlic Potatoes and Herbed Pan Sauce (15 mins active; 30 mins total) • *A steakhouse-style steak with a butter-basted exterior* page 169

Portuguese Pork Chops and Rice (20 mins active; 40 mins total) • *Throw garlic and lemon wedges into the basting butter for another dimension of flavor* page 171

Middle Eastern Beef with Lentils (35 mins active; 120 mins total) • *Build in subtle seasoning by marinating the meat before searing* page 175

Marinated Lamb with Pita and Hummus
(30 mins active; 120 mins total) • *Turn up the spicing in the marinade and pair gamy lamb with a hit of hummus* page 177

Gyoza (30 mins active; 30 mins total) • *Not just for starters anymore* page 181

Breaded Fish Fillets with Broccoli (20 mins active; 30 mins total) • *For the fish-stick-lover in everyone* page 183

Tonkatsu Chicken with Caramelized Carrots
(20 mins active; 40 mins total) • *Take your breading game in a Japanese direction* page 187

Danny's Fried Chicken with Spiced Rice
(25 mins active; 60 mins total) • *The breading two-step: battered, shallow-fried, and baked* page 189

HANDS-OFF ROASTING

Roasted Baby Back Ribs and Sweet Potatoes
(10 mins active; 80 mins total) • *Could. Not. Be. Simpler.* page 193

Roast Chicken and Potatoes with Garlic and Thyme
(10 mins active; 120 mins total) • *The quintessential comfort meal, now and forever* page 195

Porchetta Pork Belly with Truffles (25 mins active; 90 mins total) • *A new take on the Sunday roast, stuffed and rolled* page 199

Beef-Glazed Celery Root with Buttermilk Sauce
(40 mins active; 80 mins total) • *The ultimate veg roast, with savory pan juices spooned over* page 201

Pan-Roasted Cauliflower with Sesame Crème Fraîche (20 mins active; 30 mins total) • *Roasting a vegetable as you would a large cut of meat* page 205

LOW AND SLOW

Mussels with Chorizo (30 mins active; 40 mins total) • *Toss quick-cooking shellfish into a gently simmered, creamy sauce* page 207

Braised Pork Cheek Ragu (20 mins active; 4 hours total) • *A lighter, brighter pork pot roast* page 211

My Mother's Chicken Curry (60 mins active; 3 hours total) • *A homemade spice paste makes all the difference here* page 213

Lamb Curry with Rice and Raita (60 mins active; 3 hours total) • *A bolder take on curry with a creamy cashew enrichment and bits of lamb* page 217

BAKED SALMON
WITH THYME AND THIN POTATOES

SERVES 4

Cooking salmon on a bed of paper-thin potato slices is both efficient and delicious: as the fish cooks it infuses the potatoes with flavor. Make sure to buy the fish in one big piece, like a roast with the skin on; pre-portioned pieces of fish will cook too quickly and be done before the potatoes are tender. All you need to make this a meal is a green vegetable. Wild-caught salmon is always preferred to farmed fish, but in a simple preparation like this it really makes a difference.

Small Yukon Gold potatoes	1¼ pounds (570 g)
Garlic cloves	4
Extra-virgin olive oil	3 tablespoons
Fine sea salt	
Skin-on salmon fillet	1½ pounds (680 g), in 1 piece, preferably wild
Fresh thyme sprigs	4

1. Preheat the oven to 375°F (190°C).

2. Scrub the potatoes well under cold running water, but don't peel them. Using a mandoline or plastic V-slicer, cut the potatoes into paper-thin rounds.

   If you have good knife skills, you can slice the potatoes by hand, but using a slicer is a better way to get the thin, consistent slices you want here.

3. Cut the unpeeled garlic in half lengthwise. Put the potato slices and garlic on a large, rimmed baking sheet. Drizzle with half of the oil, toss well with your hands, and spread out on the sheet as thinly as possible. Drizzle with the remaining oil and season with the salt.

4. Pat the salmon dry with paper towels. Run your fingers over the flesh side to detect the protruding ends of any thin white pin bones. Use your fingers or heavy tweezers to pull out and discard the bones. Season the flesh side with

recipe continues ▸

salt. Place the salmon skin side up on top of the potatoes. Scatter the thyme over the salmon and potatoes.

Be sure to put the fish with the skin side up—the skin will help you determine when the fish is ready.

5. Roast the salmon until the skin comes off easily when pulled with kitchen tongs, about 20 minutes. Start checking for doneness after about 15 minutes, but do so at the thicker end of the fish because the thinner, tail end will be done first.

If the skin does not come off easily, just keep checking every few minutes until it does.

6. To serve, remove and discard the skin and cut the salmon into serving portions. Season with salt and serve with the potatoes.

SALT-CRUSTED SEA BASS
WITH GREEN BEANS

SERVES 4

*Whenever I can use the oven to make dinner, I do, because whether I'm roasting a chicken,
or vegetables, or a big cut of meat, the food cooks evenly without supervision, letting
me do other things while dinner is under way. Cooking sea bass under a salt crust takes
roasting a step up, literally baking flavor and a bit of color (from the turmeric) right into
the fish. It looks so impressive when you bring it to the table, but it's really not hard to
make at all, and it's fun to crack open the salt shell, releasing an amazing fragrance.*

Kosher salt or coarse sea salt	2½ cups
Unbleached all-purpose flour	½ cup (70 g)
Sweet paprika	1 teaspoon
Ground turmeric	1 teaspoon
Red pepper flakes	½ teaspoon
Large egg whites	2 to 3
Whole sea bass or red snapper	1 (3½- to 4½-pound/1.6- to 2-kg) fish gutted and cleaned, but with skin and scales
Garlic cloves	2
Salted butter	½ cup (110 g) plus 2 tablespoons
Fresh thyme sprigs	4
Green beans	1 pound (455 g)
Lemon	1

1. Preheat the oven to 400°F (200°C).

2. Mix the salt, flour, paprika, turmeric, and red pepper flakes in a large bowl.
   One at a time, stir in the egg whites to moisten the salt evenly.

   *Add just enough egg white to create a mixture that holds together with little or no crumbling
   when you squeeze a bit in your hand.*

recipe continues ▸

3. Spread about one-third of the salt mixture on a large rimmed baking sheet in a rectangle just large enough to act as a base for the fish. Wipe the inside and outside of the fish with paper towels. Crush the garlic cloves with the flat side of your knife and discard the papery skins. Cut ½ cup (110 g) of the butter into small pieces and slip them inside the fish along with the garlic and thyme sprigs. Place the fish on the baking sheet and cover it with the remaining salt mixture, patting it in place and enclosing the fish entirely.

4. Bake for 30 to 35 minutes, or until an instant-read thermometer inserted in the thickest part of the fish reads 120° to 125°F (48° to 52°C). Let the fish rest in the crust for 10 minutes before you crack the crust.

5. When the fish has been in the oven for about 20 minutes, bring about 1 quart (960 ml) water to a boil. Trim the ends off the green beans. Add the 2 tablespoons butter to the water and let it melt. Stir in the green beans and cook until they turn a deeper, richer shade of green, about 3 minutes. Using tongs or a sieve, lift the green beans from the water and transfer to a serving bowl.

   You can reuse the butter water to cook vegetables within a day or two if you wish.

6. Cut the lemon into wedges. To serve the fish, crack the top crust with the back of a large spoon and pull off as much of the salt crust as you can.

SERVING NOTES

Don't be intimidated by cooking or serving a whole fish; there is really nothing to it. I remember seeing a waiter portion a whole fish tableside for the first time and thinking, "Huh, that's easier than carving a chicken." And it is! Buy your fish with the scales on if you can, as this protects the fish from getting too salty.

Using the side of a spoon, scrape up one corner of the skin near the head and pull away the skin with your fingers to expose the flesh. Using 2 spoons, loosen and lift serving-sized portions of the flesh away from the skeleton and transfer them to dinner plates. Grab the tail and smoothly lift off the spine and head, leaving a second fillet behind. Use the spoons to cut and serve the bottom layer, avoiding the salt beneath it. Portion into fillets and serve with the lemon wedges.

BAKED COD
WITH CRUSHED TOMATOES
AND GREEN OLIVES

SERVES 4

I always feel like I'm the last one to pick up my kids from school, probably because I always think that I have more time than I actually do or that I can get from A to B faster than I really can. Copenhagen's Torvehallerne Market is practically next door to the school, and I stop in just about every day before picking them up. Of course, once I'm there I have to get a coffee, and then I bump into a friend and stop to chat for what seems like only a minute, and all of a sudden time has gotten away from me and I know I'll only have a half-hour to cook dinner when we get home. Fortunately, this baked fish takes even less time than that. It's a go-to for busy weeknights.

Cod, haddock, or scrod fillets	4 (about 7 ounces/200 g each)
Extra-virgin olive oil	5 tablespoons (75 ml)
Plum (Roma) tomatoes	4
Green olives such as Castelventrano	10
Fresh oregano sprigs	5
Fine sea salt	
Crusty bread such as ciabatta	2 slices
Garlic cloves	2

1. Preheat the oven to 350°F (180°C).

2. Pat the fish dry with paper towels. Slice off the thin side flap from each fillet, saving for another use. Coat the bottom of a baking dish large enough to hold the fish in a single layer with 2 tablespoons of the oil. Place the cod in the dish. Drizzle with another 2 tablespoons of the oil.

   You want only the thick center portion of each fillet so the fish cooks evenly and doesn't overcook.

recipe continues ▶

3. To core the tomatoes easily, slice each one downward next to but not through the stem. Make two angled cuts into the larger half to release the core and discard.

4. Squeeze each tomato half over the fish, letting the juice and seeds fall mainly on the fish. Arrange the tomatoes around the fish. Smash each of the green olives under the flat side of your knife and discard the pit. Scatter the olives over the tomatoes. Chop the oregano leaves, discarding the stems, and sprinkle over the fish and vegetables. Season very lightly with salt.

   You can choose from more delicious olive varieties if you are willing to take the pits out yourself. This technique is so easy and much quicker than using an olive pitter!

5. Tear the bread into small pieces and process into coarse crumbs in a food processor. Pour the crumbs into a medium bowl. Crush the garlic cloves with the flat side of your knife and discard the papery skins. With the machine running, drop the garlic through the feed tube of the processor to mince it. Return half of the crumbs to the processor with the remaining 1 tablespoon of oil and pulse to moisten. Add the remaining bread crumbs and pulse to combine everything. Use a spoon to sprinkle the garlic bread crumbs evenly over the fish and tomatoes.

6. Bake until the topping is golden brown and the fish flakes easily when pierced with a fork, about 15 minutes. Serve hot, right from the dish.

ROASTED RATATOUILLE WITH ORZO

SERVES 6 TO 8

It's embarrassing to admit, but I had never seen ratatouille cooked and served this way until I saw the animated film of the same name. It inspired me to revisit this dish, and I'm glad I did because when it's not cooked to a mush and the vegetables still have a bit of bite, it has the comfort and flavor of rustic food—even though it's dressed up a bit. I intensify the tomato flavor by adding even more fresh juice. It takes a bit of time to assemble, but it has real wow factor when you bring it to the table; everyone always remarks how beautiful this is. For the prettiest presentation, pick tomatoes, eggplants, and zucchini that all have a similar diameter.

Eggplant	2 narrow (about 1½ pounds/680 g total)
Zucchini	2 large (about 1 pound/455 g total)
Beefsteak tomatoes	6
Salted butter	3 tablespoons, at room temperature
Extra-virgin olive oil	4 tablespoons (60 ml)
Garlic cloves	4
Fresh thyme sprigs	8
Fresh basil leaves	3 tablespoons
Cherry tomatoes	1 pound (455 g)
Fine sea salt	
Orzo	1 pound (455 g)

1. Preheat the oven to 375°F (190°F).

2. Trim the eggplants and zucchini and slice off the stem ends of the plum tomatoes. Cut the vegetables into thin slices, about ¼ inch (6 mm) for the eggplant and zucchini, and a bit thicker for the tomatoes. Keep the vegetables separate.

   If you have a mandoline or V-slicer, use it for the eggplant and zucchini.

3. Butter a 9- to 10-inch (23- to 25-cm) round shallow casserole or a skillet with a lid with 1 tablespoon of the butter. Drizzle in 2 tablespoons of the oil.

recipe continues ▸

Crush the garlic with the flat side of your knife, then peel the garlic (discard the papery skins) and add it to the casserole along with the thyme sprigs and basil leaves. Halve the cherry tomatoes and gently squeeze them over the baking dish to release their juices and seeds into the pan. Reserve the cherry tomatoes for another use (see sidebar). Using your fingertip, poke out the seed clusters from the sliced beefsteak tomatoes and add them to the baking dish.

I use an enameled cast-iron casserole for this dish because it is heavy and distributes the heat so well. You can also use a heavy skillet, as long as the handles are ovenproof.

4. Alternate the tomato, eggplant, and zucchini slices in the baking dish in rows, filling the dish all the way to the center. Drizzle with the remaining 2 tablespoons oil and season with salt.

5. Bake uncovered for 20 minutes. Cover the casserole and continue baking until the eggplant is a few shades darker, like a strong café latte, and the zucchini is an almost translucent, pale and glossy yellowish color, 20 to 30 minutes more.

If your baking dish doesn't have a lid, place a baking sheet or even a pie tin on top.

6. While the ratatouille is baking, bring a large pot of water to a boil over high heat for the orzo. When the water boils, add a tablespoon or so of salt. Stir in the pasta and cook, stirring every 2 minutes to ensure that it does not stick to the bottom, and cook according to the package directions until al dente, about 8 minutes, depending on the brand.

7. To warm the pasta serving bowl, place it in the sink and set a colander inside. Drain the pasta in the colander and return it to the cooking pot, letting the hot pasta water stand in the serving bowl for about 30 seconds to warm it. Empty and dry the serving bowl and add the pasta. Stir in the remaining 2 tablespoons of butter.

8. To serve, bring the ratatouille to the table in its baking dish. Spoon the orzo into bowls and top each serving with the ratatouille and some of its juices.

REDUCING KITCHEN WASTE

I hate to throw anything usable and edible away, and instead think of these odds and ends as a head start on future meals. The squeezed-out cherry tomatoes can be mixed with some diced onion, fresh chile, cilantro, olive oil, and lime juice for a quick salsa to put on cooked fish or a cheese omelet, or you can chop and combine them with basil, garlic, salt, and red pepper flakes for an uncooked sauce to toss with hot pasta and cubes of mozzarella.

EGGPLANT GRATIN

SERVES 9 TO 12

My inspiration for this dish comes from watching a video clip on the Franks—Frank Castronovo and Frank Falcinelli—making an eggplant parm sandwich. It's a cross between eggplant parm and a traditional lasagna, although it's made without béchamel or heavy mozzarella. It's really good warm from the oven, but I like it even better at room temperature, especially in hot weather. You can fry the eggplant while the sauce simmers, or even earlier in the day if you like, because the slices will reheat when you bake them with the sauce.

TOMATO SAUCE

Garlic cloves	5
Extra-virgin olive oil	3 tablespoons
Crushed tomatoes	2 (28-ounce/784-g) cans
Fine sea salt	

Eggplants	3 large (4 pounds/1.8 kg total)
Fine sea salt	
Canola oil	1 quart (960 ml), as needed, for deep-frying
Unbleached all-purpose flour	1½ cups (210 g) or as needed
Freshly ground black pepper	
Large eggs	8 or 9
Pecorino Romano cheese	1¼ cups (140 g) freshly grated
Parmigiano-Reggiano cheese	2½ cups (275 g) freshly grated

1. **Make the tomato sauce:** Heat a large saucepan over low heat. Crush the garlic cloves under the flat side of a knife and peel the garlic. Add the olive oil to the saucepan, then the garlic. Cook the garlic until golden brown, about 2 minutes, then stir in the tomatoes. Bring to a simmer over high heat, then reduce the heat to medium. Simmer, stirring frequently, until the sauce has reduced by one-third, about 30 minutes. Season with the salt. Remove from the heat and discard the garlic.

recipe continues ▶

2. Cut the eggplants lengthwise into slices about ½ inch (12 mm) thick. Lightly sprinkle on both sides with salt and lay the slices on paper towels. Let stand for about 15 minutes. Wipe dry with the towels.

3. Pour enough oil into a large deep skillet to come halfway up the sides and heat it over medium heat until it is shimmering.

   Use the end of a wooden spoon to see when the oil has the correct temperature—when the oil starts to bubble around the spoon, the oil is hot enough.

4. Line a baking sheet with paper towels. Carefully slide 3 slices of the eggplant into the hot oil (preferably with silicone-tipped tongs, which won't pierce the eggplant). Push the slices under the oil and fry until softened slightly, about 2 minutes. Move them to the paper towels to drain. Repeat with the remaining eggplant slices, cooking them in batches. Let the eggplant cool for at least 5 minutes. Reduce the heat under the oil to very low but do not turn it off.

   The idea here is to partially cook the eggplant, not cook it all the way through. It will cook through when it is coated and fried.

5. Put the flour in a wide, shallow bowl. Season with salt and pepper. Whisk the eggs in a second shallow bowl and whisk in the Romano cheese and 1 cup (110 g) of the Parmigiano cheese to combine. Raise the heat under the oil to medium-high again. One at a time, coat an eggplant slice evenly in the flour, then in the egg and cheese mixture. Carefully slide 2 to 4 eggplant slices into the hot oil. Fry, turning once, until golden brown on both sides, about 1½ minutes. Use a slotted spatula or the silicone-tipped tongs to transfer the eggplant to the paper towels. Repeat with the remaining eggplant slices.

   You can fry as many slices as fit comfortably in the pan but don't crowd it.

6. Spread a thin layer of the tomato sauce in the bottom of a 9 × 13-inch (23 × 33-cm) baking dish. Casually layer the eggplant and sauce in the dish (this doesn't have to be precise) ending with a layer of sauce. Sprinkle with the remaining 1 cup (110 g) Parmigiano cheese.

7. Bake until the sauce is bubbling and the cheese is melted, about 45 minutes. Let stand at room temperature for 10 minutes or cool to room temperature. Cut into squares and serve.

"SEAL THE DEAL" PASTA

SERVES 4 TO 6

*We jokingly gave this pasta its name because it's what René made for me on our first
date. It's a bit more sophisticated than my everyday tomato sauce—the tomatoes are
peeled, for example, although in reality this is not as much extra work as you'd think.
That little refinement makes a big difference though. The beurre blanc sauce is silky
smooth and downright seductive, so I guess it truly does earn its name. For a simple
sauce like this, I like the flavor of dry vermouth, and always have a bottle in the pantry.
Unlike white wine, it can stay on the shelf almost indefinitely, so when you need
only a small amount, as here, you don't need to open up a whole bottle.*

Ripe plum (Roma) tomatoes	1¾ pounds (800 g)
Fresh basil leaves	25 large leaves
Coarse sea salt	1 tablespoon
Penne rigate	1 pound
Flaky sea salt	
Cold salted butter	¾ cup (165 g)
Dry white vermouth	¾ cup (180 ml)

1. Bring a large pot of water to a boil. Using a small, sharp knife, cut a shallow X
   in the skin on the bottom of each tomato. One at a time, add the tomatoes
   to the water and cook just until the skin loosens, about 10 seconds (or longer,
   depending on how ripe the tomatoes are). Using a slotted spoon, transfer
   each tomato to a large bowl. When the tomatoes are cool enough to handle,
   use the small knife to peel off the skins. Save the water for cooking the pasta.

   *If your tomatoes are not very ripe, it may take a few extra seconds in the boiling water to
   loosen the skins.*

2. Halve the tomatoes lengthwise. Working over a small bowl, use your fingertip
   to poke out the seeds and gel. (Save them for another use.) Chop the tomato
   flesh into ½-inch (12-mm) pieces. Coarsely chop the basil.

recipe continues ▸

3. Bring the pot of water back to a boil and add the fine sea salt. Stir in the pasta and cook, stirring every 2 minutes, until the pasta is al dente, about 8 minutes, depending on the brand.

4. **While the pasta cooks, make the beurre blanc sauce:** Cut the butter into small cubes. Bring the vermouth to a boil in a small saucepan over high heat and cook until reduced to ¼ cup, about 2 minutes. Turn the heat down as low as it will go. A few at a time, whisk in the butter cubes, letting the butter soften into a thick sauce without actually melting. Keep adding bits of butter, moving the pan off the heat now and then so it can cool slightly, until all of the cubes have been incorporated and the sauce is smooth. Stir in the tomatoes and basil and remove from the heat.

   You're not melting the butter here, just getting it warm enough to become fluid but still opaque. Take your time and don't overheat the butter.

5. Place the pasta serving bowl in the sink and set a colander inside. Drain the pasta into the colander. Return the pasta to its cooking pot and let the water stand in the bowl for a minute to warm it. Empty and dry the serving bowl and add the pasta. Add the sauce to the pasta and mix gently but thoroughly. Season with flaky salt and transfer to the warmed serving dish.

6. Serve immediately in bowls, being sure to reach all the way to the bottom of the serving bowl to scoop up the sauce.

SPAGHETTI
WITH FRESH TOMATO AND BASIL SAUCE

SERVES 4

I've been making and refining this recipe for more than a decade, and I finally feel I've gotten it just right. It's an all-purpose tomato sauce you can use for countless pasta dishes as well as pizza, layered dishes like eggplant gratin on page 108, and more. Depending on the end use, you might want to add some cooked sausage or even bacon to the sauce, letting it simmer with the tomatoes after you break them up. I make this with beefsteak tomatoes when they are in season; the rest of the year Roma (plum) tomatoes work wonderfully.

Extra-virgin olive oil	10 tablespoons (150 ml)
Onion	1 large
Garlic cloves	5
Coarse sea salt	
Large, meaty tomatoes such as beefsteak or plum (Roma)	3 pounds (1.4 kg)
Fresh basil leaves	1 cup (40 g) packed
Salted butter	2 tablespoons
Parmigiano-Reggiano cheese	1 cup (110 g) freshly grated, plus more for serving
Spaghetti	1 pound (455 g)

1. Heat 4 tablespoons (60 ml) of the oil in a large skillet over medium heat.

2. Chop the onion and add it to the skillet. Cook without stirring until it begins to brown, about 2 minutes. Now give the onion a stir, reduce the heat to medium, and cook until it caramelizes to a deep golden brown, 8 to 10 minutes, stirring frequently. Crush the garlic cloves under the flat side of a knife, peel the garlic, and discard the papery skins. Stir the garlic into the pan. Season with salt and reduce the heat to medium-low. Stir in 2 tablespoons of water and cook until it has evaporated, about 3 minutes. Repeat the process, adding water and cooking it down until the mixture has an almost jam-like consistency, 8 to 10 minutes more.

recipe continues ▸

3. To core the tomatoes easily, slice downward next to but not through the stem. Make two angled cuts into the larger half to release the core and discard. Slice the tomato lengthwise and vertically, and then coarsely chop the slices into coarse dice.

   Yes, I include the skin and seeds. I find this gives the sauce more flavor!

4. Add the tomatoes to the pan and reduce the heat to very low. Add a little more salt and another 2 tablespoons of the oil. Cook until the tomatoes soften, about 10 minutes.

5. Use a potato masher to crush the tomatoes into a smooth sauce right in the pan. Stir in another 2 tablespoons of oil. Simmer, stirring occasionally, until thickened, 30 to 40 minutes. Toward the end of the sauce's cooking time, bring a large pot of water to a boil over high heat.

   By this point, most of the tomato skin will have broken down, but if you really do not like the texture of the skin, fish out any visible pieces with tongs.

6. Chop the basil. Add the butter and half of the basil to the sauce and stir until the butter is incorporated. Gradually stir in the 1 cup (110 g) Parmigiano and the remaining 2 tablespoons oil. Remove from the heat.

   I like to let the sauce stand while cooking the pasta because I find that the extra time helps build more flavor.

7. Add a tablespoon or so of salt to the boiling pasta water. Stir in the pasta and cook according to the package directions, stirring occasionally, until al dente, about 8 minutes, depending on the brand.

8. Reheat the sauce, if necessary. Drain the pasta and transfer it to individual bowls. Top each with a big spoonful of the tomato sauce. Serve hot with the remaining basil and additional Parmigiano.

PASTA WITH MEAT SAUCE

SERVES 4 TO 6

A heartier counterpart to my basic tomato sauce, this can be made year-round with good-quality canned organic tomatoes. I've learned that when it comes to this kind of sauce, everyone has strong opinions that are probably influenced by the sauce they grew up eating. I usually omit the wine because I don't feel this sauce needs the extra acidity, and I add a second infusion of garlic near the end of cooking because, in my opinion, there can never be enough garlic in a meat sauce. Tasting and tweaking the seasoning along the way is what will make this sauce truly your own.

Extra-virgin olive oil	12 tablespoons (180 ml)
Onions	2 medium
Garlic cloves	8, plus more to taste
Ground round (85 percent lean)	1 pound (455 g)
Hearty red wine	½ cup (120 ml) (optional)
Whole peeled plum tomatoes in juice	1 (28-ounce/784-g) can
Beef stock	½ cup (120 ml)
Tomato paste	2 tablespoons
Extra-virgin olive oil	½ cup (120 ml)
Coarse sea salt	
Penne pasta	1 pound (455 g)
Fresh basil leaves	30
Parmigiano-Reggiano cheese	1 cup (55 g), freshly grated, plus more for serving

1. Heat 4 tablespoons (60 ml) of the oil in a Dutch oven or large, heavy saucepan over medium-high heat. Chop the onions, adding half an onion to the pot as you go. When all of the onions have been added, let them cook, stirring occasionally, until they turn a deep golden brown, about 5 minutes. Crush the 8 garlic cloves under the flat blade of a knife, discard the papery skins, and peel and chop the garlic (it doesn't have to be minced), and stir it into the pot.

recipe continues ▸

2. Push the onion mixture over to one side. Add 2 more tablespoons of the olive oil. Crumble the ground meat into the pot, and let it brown without stirring for a minute, then break it up with a wooden spatula. Stir the meat and onion mixture together. Let it brown for a minute more and stir again. Repeat until the meat is browned, about 6 minutes. Stir in the wine, if using, and let it come to a boil.

3. Add the tomatoes and the juice with the stock. Stir, breaking up the tomatoes with the spatula, and bring to a boil. Reduce the heat to medium-low and cook at a steady simmer for 30 to 40 minutes, stirring occasionally, until the liquid has reduced by about one-fourth. Stir in the tomato paste, followed by the remaining 6 tablespoons (90 ml) oil, and continue simmering until the sauce is thick and rich, about 20 minutes more.

   Adding a bit more olive oil at this stage gives the sauce extra body.

4. Bring a large pot of water to a boil over high heat. Add a tablespoon or so of salt. Stir in the pasta and cook, stirring every 2 minutes, according to the package directions until the pasta is al dente, about 8 minutes.

5. Set the pasta serving bowl in the sink and set a colander inside. Drain the pasta into the colander. Return the pasta to its cooking pot and let the water stand in the serving bowl to warm it.

6. Remove the sauce from the heat. Coarsely chop the basil into a serving bowl. In two batches, stir the Parmigiano into the sauce, along with half of the basil. Taste the sauce and season with salt and pepper. Add more garlic to taste, if you like.

7. Empty and dry the serving bowl and add the pasta. Top with the meat sauce. Pass the remaining basil and additional Parmigiano with the pasta so diners can season their servings to taste.

SPAGHETTI WITH MUSSEL SAUCE

SERVES 4

My obsession with watching cooking shows probably dates back to a time I was home and sick in bed as a young girl. Bored, I was looking for anything to watch on TV besides an endless marathon of Days of Our Lives *reruns when I stumbled across an Italian chef called Antonio Carluccio. Seeing him prepare a pasta sauce with fresh seafood in the beautiful Italian countryside made me hungry for the first time in days. I wrote down whatever I could remember from the show and tried to re-create it, and I've been making a version of that recipe ever since, though it has changed quite a bit.*

Onions	3
Dry white wine	1 (750-ml) bottle
Fresh thyme sprigs	2
Bay leaf	1
Mussels	2¼ pounds (1 kg)
Extra-virgin olive oil	6 tablespoons (90 ml)
Garlic cloves	5
Crushed tomatoes	1 (28-ounce/784-g) can
Salted butter	¼ cup (60 g)
Capers	⅓ cup (50 g)
Flaky sea salt	
Coarse sea salt	
Spaghetti	1 pound (455 g)
Fresh flat-leaf parsley leaves	¼ cup (20 g) finely chopped

1. Cut off the top and bottom of one of the onions. Peel the onion, cut it in half lengthwise, and then cut it into thin half-moons. Bring the wine, sliced onion, thyme, and bay leaf to a boil in a large pot over high heat. Add the mussels and cover the pot tightly. Cook for 5 minutes, occasionally giving the pot a good shake. Check to see if the mussels have opened. If not, cover and cook another minute or so, until almost all are open. Empty the mussels into a colander set inside a large bowl to collect the cooking liquid.

   If any of the mussels have not opened by this point, you should discard them.

recipe continues ▸

2. Pour the cooking liquid into a saucepan and boil over high heat until reduced by half—this should take about 10 minutes. As it reduces, remove the mussels from their shells and discard the shells, working over a bowl to collect any additional juices.

3. Chop the remaining 2 onions. Rinse out the pot that held the mussels and heat it over medium-high heat. Add 2 tablespoons of the olive oil and, when it's very hot but not smoking, add the chopped onions. Cook without stirring until they begin to brown, about 2 minutes. Give them a stir and continue cooking until they are golden brown, about 3 minutes more.

    If you let the onions get some color on them before you stir them, they will caramelize better.

4. Crush the garlic cloves under the flat side of your knife, discard the papery skins, and peel and chop the cloves. Stir the garlic into the pot, then mix in the tomatoes and butter. Bring the sauce to a simmer. Add the reduced cooking liquid and the capers, stir to combine, then turn the heat down to low. Simmer the sauce, stirring occasionally, until nice and thick, about 30 minutes. Season to taste with flaky salt. Stir in the remaining 4 tablespoons (60 ml) olive oil. Keep the sauce warm over very low heat.

5. While the sauce is simmering, bring a large pot of water to a boil over high heat. Add a tablespoon or so of coarse salt. Stir in the pasta and cook, stirring occasionally, according to the package directions until al dente, about 8 minutes.

6. Place the pasta serving bowl in the sink and set a colander inside. Drain the pasta in the colander, then return it to the cooking pot. Let the hot pasta water stand in the serving bowl for about 30 seconds to warm it.

7. Stir the shelled mussels and any juices into the warm sauce. Add the pasta to the warmed bowl, ladle the mussel sauce over the pasta, and mix gently. Sprinkle with the chopped parsley, toss one more time, and serve.

ROTINI WITH SPICY CHICKEN LIVER SAUCE

SERVES 4 TO 6

Inexpensive, readily available chicken livers have fallen out of fashion, which I think is a shame. In Portugal, where I was born, all the local families raised chickens and geese to sell, and it was traditional to keep the chicken livers for family meals. In a rich sauce like this, they contribute a savory, meaty flavor, the way anchovies might. Stirring in a bit of olive oil at the end adds richness and binds the elements of the sauce together. One teaspoon may seem like a lot of cayenne, but the livers really mellow the heat. If you like this really spicy (as I do), you could use as much as an extra half-teaspoon of cayenne, but proceed with caution; you can always add a bit more just before serving. The first time I cooked for René, I immediately knew this was the dish I wanted to make, but I was afraid that as a chef he would not approve of canned tomatoes, so I used fresh. Big mistake: it isn't the same dish at all with fresh tomatoes.

Chicken livers	12 ounces (340 g)
Canola oil	2 tablespoons
Garlic cloves	4
Ground cayenne	1 teaspoon, or to taste
Sweet paprika	1 teaspoon
Smoked paprika	1 teaspoon
Whole peeled plum tomatoes in juice	1 (28-ounce/784-g) can
Tomato paste	2 tablespoons
Extra-virgin olive oil	3 tablespoons
Coarse sea salt	
Freshly ground black pepper	
Rotini	1 pound (455 g)
Fresh flat-leaf parsley leaves	¼ cup (20 g)

1. Spread the livers on paper towels and pat them dry. Trim the livers and cut them into 3 or 4 pieces.

    Handling the raw livers takes some getting used to—hang in there. Just remove any veins with a small, sharp knife.

recipe continues ▸

2. Heat the canola oil in a large skillet over medium-high heat. Crush the garlic cloves with the flat side of a knife, discard the papery skins, then peel and chop the garlic. Add the cayenne pepper, sweet paprika, and smoked paprika to the oil and stir, then add the garlic. Immediately remove the pan from the heat and let the garlic warm in the hot oil for about 30 seconds, or until fragrant.

   This is a super-gentle to way to cook garlic without burning it, which can spoil your whole dish.

3. Return the pan to the heat. Add the livers in a single layer. Let them cook without moving them until they are brown on the underside, about 2 minutes. Remove the pan from the heat and swirl it to mix the juices. Return to the heat, turn the livers, and brown on the second side for about 2 minutes more.

   Don't crowd the chicken livers in the center of the pan, or they won't brown properly and will give off too much liquid.

4. Add the tomatoes with their juices and the tomato paste to the skillet and stir with a wooden spoon to loosen any browned bits in the bottom of the skillet and break up the tomatoes. Bring to a simmer, then stir in the olive oil and season to taste with salt and pepper. Reduce the heat to medium-low and simmer, stirring every few minutes, until the sauce has thickened slightly and the livers are just cooked through, 10 to 15 minutes.

   Don't let this simmer too long; the texture of the livers becomes grainy and crumbly when overcooked.

5. Bring a large pot of water to a boil over high heat. Add a tablespoon or so of coarse salt. Stir in the pasta and cook, stirring every 2 minutes, according to the package directions until the pasta is al dente, about 8 minutes, depending on the brand.

6. Place the pasta serving bowl in the sink and set a colander inside. Drain the pasta in the colander, then return it to the cooking pot. Let the hot pasta water stand in the serving bowl for about 30 seconds to warm it. Empty and dry the serving bowl and add the pasta.

7. Spoon about one-fourth of the sauce into the serving bowl. Add the pasta and top with the remaining sauce. Coarsely chop the parsley and sprinkle it over the pasta. Mix at the table and serve immediately.

LASAGNA WITH SAUSAGE MEATBALLS

SERVES 9 TO 12

When it was our oldest daughter's turn to have her school playgroup over for dinner, I asked her what she wanted me to make and she requested lasagna. I've never been a huge fan of lasagna, which is usually a bit bland and stuffed with too much melted cheese for my taste, so I challenged myself to create a version that was full of flavor and a bit surprising. I added a lot of garlic and little balls of sausage in addition to the ground beef, and layered in a lightly cheesy béchamel sauce, and it really took it to the next level for me. This requires a bit of work, but it serves a big crowd.

MEAT SAUCE

Extra-virgin olive oil	6 tablespoons (90 ml)
Onions	2
Garlic cloves	8
Ground beef chuck (about 80 percent lean)	1¾ pounds (800 g)
Whole peeled tomatoes in juice	3 (14½-ounce/406-g) cans
Fine sea salt	
Freshly ground black pepper	

BÉCHAMEL

Salted butter	½ cup (110 g)
Unbleached all-purpose flour	½ cup (70 g)
Whole milk	4 cups (950 ml)
Fine sea salt	
Sweet Italian pork sausage	1 pound (455 g)
No-boil pasta sheets	1 (1-pound/450-g) box
Parmigiano-Reggiano cheese	2 cups (225 g) freshly grated

1. **Make the meat sauce:** Heat 2 tablespoons of the oil in a large Dutch oven over medium-high heat. Chop the onions, adding them to the pot as you go. Do not stir until the onions are beginning to brown, about 2 minutes. Cook,

recipe continues ▸

stirring occasionally, until they turn a deep golden brown, about 3 minutes more. Crush the garlic cloves with the flat side of your knife and discard the papery skins. Coarsely chop the garlic and stir it into the pot.

2. Push the onion mixture to one side of the pot and add 2 more tablespoons of the oil. Crumble the ground beef into the pot, avoiding the onions. Let the meat cook for 2 minutes to lightly brown on the bottom. Using a wooden spatula, break up the meat and stir it into the onions. Cook, stirring occasionally, until the meat is browned, about 8 minutes. Add the tomatoes with their juices and stir to combine, crushing the tomatoes with the spatula.

3. Simmer the sauce until thickened slightly, about 40 minutes, stirring now and then. Stir in the remaining 2 tablespoons oil. Season to taste with salt and pepper.

   Stirring in a bit of extra oil will help emulsify the sauce and give it more body.

4. Preheat the oven to 350°F (180°C).

5. **Make the béchamel:** Melt the butter in a large saucepan over medium-low heat. Gradually whisk in the flour to make a thick, paste-like roux. Let it bubble for about a minute but don't let it brown. Raise the heat to medium. Gradually whisk in the milk. Simmer over medium-low heat, whisking often and making sure the bottom doesn't scorch, until it is lightly thickened and smooth, about 10 minutes. Remove from the heat and season with salt.

6. Place a large skillet over medium-high heat. Squeeze the sausage meat out of the casings, forming it into small balls with your fingers. Add them to the skillet and cook until they are lightly browned and their fat has rendered. Use a slotted spoon to transfer them to the sauce and combine gently.

7. Spread about 1 cup (240 ml) of the meat sauce in a 9 x 13-inch (23 x 33-cm) baking dish. Top with a layer of lasagna sheets. Cover with about one-fourth of the remaining meat sauce, one-fourth of the béchamel, and sprinke with ½ cup (55 g) of the Parmigiano. Repeat to make 3 more layers. (You may have extra lasagna sheets.) Sprinkle with the remaining Parmigiano.

   You can break the lasagna sheets to get them to fit perfectly, if necessary.

8. Bake the lasagna until it is bubbling and browned, about 50 minutes. Remove from the oven and let stand for at least 20 minutes before serving.

   Don't cut into the lasagna too soon, or it will fall apart when you serve it. Even 20 minutes isn't too long a resting period, and it will still be hot.

DUCK BREAST RICE BOWL
WITH TOMATOES AND CUCUMBERS

SERVES 4

Duck is one of those meats people seem to save for "fancy" occasions, but it really deserves a spot in your weeknight rotation. It's as easy to cook as a steak, but more delicate than beef or pork, and because it is rich you won't eat a massive amount. This slow-cooking method renders the fat and cooks the meat to a perfect medium-rare; our girls are crazy for the crispy skin. Though not strictly authentic, this Asian-inspired dish is a nice and very easy way to pull together a weeknight meal. I've tossed in cucumbers and tomatoes, things I always have on hand for the kids, but spinach, Chinese broccoli, or red cabbage would be pretty, delicious additions. Don't omit the cucumber, as it adds a pleasing crunch. Look for a good-quality organic soy sauce, because it is the predominant seasoning here.

Long-grain or jasmine rice	2 cups (400 g)
Boneless duck breasts (maigrets)	2 (about 1 pound/455 g each)
Fine sea salt	
Cucumber	1
Tomatoes	2
Fresh basil leaves	20 large
Chicken broth	½ cup (120 ml)
Soy sauce	1 tablespoon, plus more for serving
Extra-virgin olive oil	For serving

1. **Start by making the rice:** Combine 4 cups (960 ml) water and the rice in a medium saucepan. Stir to combine, then bring to a boil over medium heat. Reduce the heat to low, cover the saucepan, and cook without disturbing until little air pockets appear on the top of the rice, about 15 minutes. Remove from the heat and let stand, covered, for 10 to 15 minutes.

   Don't stir the rice once it is simmering, as that will make it sticky and lumpy.

recipe continues ▸

CONGRATULATIONS: YOU MADE A RICE BOWL

This is just one example of how to combine proteins and veggies served on a bed of rice. It's nice to make fresh ones, like this duck bowl, where the topping is hot and you can make a little pan sauce, but rice bowls are also a great way to use leftovers—and I do exactly that many nights when I am pressed for time. Any cooked grain could stand in for the rice, and you could use whatever bits of cooked meat or leftover roasted or chopped raw vegetables you have on hand. Just make sure the rice or other grain is warm, and drizzle everything with the dressing to unify the flavors. Here are some possible combos:

• Grilled steak with cherry tomatoes on brown rice
• Cooked sausages with sautéed kale on farro
• Roast lamb and roasted vegetables on couscous with harissa
• Baked salmon and baby spinach leaves on bulgur with lemon

2. Once the rice is simmering, move on to the duck. Using a very sharp knife, cut a crosshatch pattern into the skin and fat (but not the meat) of each breast, making the cuts about 1 inch (2.5 cm) apart. Put the duck breast halves in a large, dry skillet, skin side down. Place the skillet over medium heat and cook, letting the duck slowly release its fat as it cooks, and without turning the breasts, until the skin is crisp and golden brown, 12 to 15 minutes. You can tell the breast is ready to be flipped when a few drops of blood have risen to the surface of the meat.

   It's important to start with a cold, dry pan. If the pan is hot, the skin will get brown before the fat is fully rendered.

3. Flip the duck breasts over and cook until an instant-read thermometer inserted vertically to the center of the meat reads 120° to 125°F (48° to 52°C) for medium-rare (the duck will continue to cook as it rests), about 7 minutes. Transfer the breasts to a cutting board, skin side up. Sprinkle with a good pinch of salt. Let them rest for 5 to 10 minutes.

4. While the duck cooks, peel the cucumber and cut it into quarters lengthwise, then crosswise into thin pieces. To core the tomatoes easily, slice downward next to but not through the stem. Make two angled cuts into the larger half to release the core and discard. Cut the tomatoes into thin wedges. Coarsely chop the basil.

5. Pour out all of the fat in the skillet. (You can save it and use it to cook potatoes another time if you like.) Add the chicken broth and bring to a boil, scraping up the browned bits in the bottom of the pan with a wooden spatula. Boil until the broth has reduced by about one-fourth, about 1 minute. Remove from the heat and stir in the soy sauce.

6. To serve, divide the rice among 4 bowls and top with the cucumbers, tomatoes, and basil. Slice the duck about ¼ inch thick. Divide the duck among the bowls and drizzle with the pan sauce. Serve hot, with olive oil and additional soy sauce on the side for drizzling if desired.

QUINOA SALAD WITH SPICED ONIONS

SERVES 4 TO 6

Some grain salads can be a little boring, but this one is anything but. I was putting together a quick dinner of of leftover quinoa when I remembered a time Ben Shewry, a talented Australian chef who was visiting us, had suggested we bake some of the cooked grains to make them crispy. Genius idea! While the quinoa toasted, I cooked up some onions until they were dark and sweet, almost bacony, then seasoned them aggressively. The finished salad had so many different flavors and kinds of crunch! Cooked quinoa is good grain to to have in the fridge for hearty salads like this one, though even if you are starting from scratch this doesn't take long to assemble. Vadouvan is similar to a garam masala made with lots of onions and shallots. If you can't find it, substitute garam masala.

Quinoa	1 cup (200 g)
Fine sea salt	

SPICED ONIONS

Onions	3 large
Canola oil	2 tablespoons
Salted butter	3 tablespoons
Vadouvan spice blend	4 teaspoons

Extra-virgin olive oil	¼ cup (60 ml) plus 2 teaspoons
Tomatoes	2 large
Fennel	1 bulb
Red bell pepper	1
Cucumber	½
Celery	2 stalks
Scallions	3 or 4
Sugar snap peas	4 ounces (115 g)
Hass avocado	1
Lemons	2
Fresh flat-leaf parsley	30 sprigs
Fresh cilantro	30 sprigs
Freshly ground black pepper	

recipe continues ▶

1. Combine the quinoa, 2 cups (480 ml) water, and ½ teaspoon salt in a medium saucepan. Bring to a boil over high heat. Reduce the heat to low and cover with the lid slightly askew. Simmer until the quinoa is tender and has absorbed the water, about 20 minutes. Remove from the heat and set aside, covered, for 5 minutes. Uncover and let cool. Using a fork, fluff the quinoa into a bowl.

   Don't be tempted to stir quinoa as it cooks; this can make it lumpy.

2. **Make the toasted quinoa.** Preheat the oven to 350°F (180°C).

3. Line a large, rimmed baking sheet with parchment paper. Toss about one-third of the cooked quinoa with the 2 teaspoons olive oil and spread it in a thin layer on the parchment. Bake until the quinoa is crispy, about 15 minutes. Let it cool on the pan while you assemble the salad.

4. **Make the spiced onions:** Cut off the top and bottom ends of the onions. Cut each in half lengthwise and peel off the skins. One at a time, place an onion half, cut side down, on the work surface and cut into thin half-moons.

5. Heat a large skillet over medium-high heat. Add the oil and heat until it is shimmering but not smoking. Add the onions and cook without stirring until they start to brown on the bottom, about 2 minutes. Stir them and cook, stirring often, until they are browned around the edges and translucent, about 5 minutes. Reduce the heat to low. A tablespoon at a time, stir in the butter, letting each addition melt into the onions before adding the next. Cook, stirring occasionally, until the onions are very tender and golden brown, about 10 minutes. Stir in the vadouvan spices and reduce the heat to its lowest setting. Cook, stirring often, for another 10 minutes, then set aside.

6. Scoop the remaining quinoa into a large serving bowl. Add the ¼ cup (60 ml) oil and toss lightly.

7. To core the tomatoes easily, slice downward next to but not through the stem. Make two angled cuts into the larger half to release the core and discard. Dice the tomatoes and add to the bowl. Halve the fennel bulb lengthwise. Cut out and discard the hard core at the bottom. Place each half cut side down and cut crosswise into thin half-moons. (Include any tender fennel stalks, too, if they are attached.) Add to the bowl.

8. Standing the bell pepper upright, cut downward to slice the four sides away from the core. Peel the cucumber, halve lengthwise, and scoop out and discard the seeds. Cut the bell pepper slabs and cucumber into ½-inch (12-mm) dice and add to the bowl. Cut each sugar snap pea crosswise in thirds. Add to the bowl. Slice the celery and scallions and add to the bowl.

9. Halve the avocados. Use the tip of the knife to thinly cut the flesh of both halves lengthwise into thin slices right in the peel. Use a large spoon to scoop the slices into the bowl. Cut the lemons in half and squeeze them over the quinoa mixture. Coarsely chop the parsley and cilantro leaves (you can use some of the thin, tender stems) and mix well, seasoning to taste with salt and pepper. Just before serving, top with the spiced onions and toasted quinoa.

BUTTERNUT SQUASH AND CARROT SOUP

SERVES 6 TO 8

Mexico is a favorite vacation destination for our family, and while we are there we often arrange to have a local woman come in to cook for us (hey, even chefs deserve a week off from cooking now and then!). One year, we were served a soup, made from a local squash, that had a big chunk of Philadelphia Cream Cheese blended into it and the kids went crazy for it. Back home, they begged me to make it, and I came up with this version that pleased their taste buds but was a bit more interesting for me. The spices add depth but are mild enough not to turn off the kids, and a bit of sour cream provides the creaminess they were looking for.

SOUP

Winter squash such as butternut	2 pounds (960 g)
Carrots	5 large
Fresh ginger	1 (1-inch/2.5-cm) piece
Extra-virgin olive oil	3 tablespoons
Onions	2
Ground turmeric	1 tablespoon
Smoked paprika	1 tablespoon
Fresh thyme sprigs	2
Chicken broth	6 cups (1.4 L)
Tomatoes	5

FRIED SAGE LEAVES

Canola oil	½ cup (120 ml)
Sage leaves	25 large

Pine nuts	3 tablespoons
Lemon	1
Sour cream	1 cup (225 ml)
Fine sea salt	
Freshly ground pepper	
Parmigiano-Reggiano cheese	1 (8-ounce/220-g) chunk
Paprika	¼ teaspoon plus more for serving

recipe continues ▸

1. **Make the soup:** Cut the squash into large chunks, discarding the seeds, and peel the chunks. Now, cut the squash into 2-inch (5-cm) chunks. Scrub the carrots and cut them into thin rounds. Peel and chop the ginger.

   You'll need a sturdy vegetable peeler to peel the squash.

2. Heat the olive oil in a large soup pot over medium heat. While the oil heats, halve the onions lengthwise and remove the skins. Chop the onions coarsely, add them to the pot, and let them brown, without stirring, for about 2 minutes. Stir and continue to cook until they are golden brown, 2 to 3 minutes. Stir in the squash, carrots, and ginger, followed by the turmeric, smoked paprika, and thyme. Stir well to coat the vegetables and lightly toast the spices. Add the broth and bring to a boil over high heat.

   Toasting the spices in the pot brings out their flavor.

3. To core the tomatoes easily, slice downward next to but not through the stem. Make two angled cuts into the larger half to release the core and discard. Coarsely chop the tomatoes. Stir the tomatoes into the soup. Reduce the heat to medium-low and simmer, uncovered, stirring occasionally, until the squash is very tender when pierced with the tip of a knife, about 45 minutes.

4. **Fry the sage leaves:** Heat the canola oil in a small saucepan over medium-high heat until the oil is shimmering but not smoking. A few at a time, add the sage leaves to the oil and cook just until they turn a darker green—this will take only a few seconds. Using the wire skimmer, transfer the leaves to a paper towel–lined plate and let them drain and crisp.

5. Heat a small, dry skillet over medium heat. Add the pine nuts and cook, shaking the pan every 20 to 30 seconds, until they are lightly toasted. Pour the nuts out onto a plate.

   Don't leave the pine nuts in the skillet or they will continue to toast and eventually burn.

6. When the squash and carrots are tender, remove the soup from the heat. Discard the thyme stems. Working in batches, purée the soup in a blender with the lid ajar until smooth, then pour it into a clean pot. Juice the lemon and add to the soup. Stir in the sour cream and season with salt and pepper.

   Do not overfill the blender, and be sure to leave the lid ajar to vent the steam!

7. Ladle the soup into bowls. Top each serving with a few shavings of Parmigiano, some sage leaves, and pine nuts. Sprinkle with paprika and pass more at the table.

YUCATÁN STEW
WITH ROASTED CHILE SALSA

SERVES 6 TO 8

In the Yucatán, it is common to combine potatoes and beans to make a super-hearty stew. My kids prefer this stripped-down version, but if you like, by all means add some chunks of carrot, summer or peeled winter squash, plantains, or your favorite sturdy greens when you add the potatoes; all would be perfectly authentic. While the soup itself is not highly seasoned, a topping of charred-chile salsa really wakes up the flavor. In Mexico, the salsa would be made with the juice of a sour orange, and if you can find one, it is extra delicious; otherwise, the lemon juice makes a perfectly good substitute. This is just the right thing for a winter kitchen supper. Serve with bread and butter, which is very un-Mexican but really good.

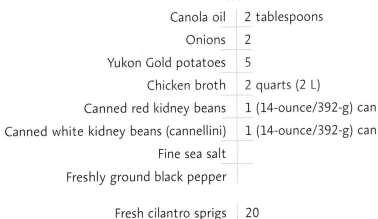

CHILE SALSA

Fresh jalapeños	6
Limes	3

SOUP

Canola oil	2 tablespoons
Onions	2
Yukon Gold potatoes	5
Chicken broth	2 quarts (2 L)
Canned red kidney beans	1 (14-ounce/392-g) can
Canned white kidney beans (cannellini)	1 (14-ounce/392-g) can
Fine sea salt	
Freshly ground black pepper	
Fresh cilantro sprigs	20
Limes	2, for serving

1. **Make the salsa:** Preheat the broiler on high with the oven rack about 6 inches (15 cm) from the heat source. Put the jalapeños in a broiler pan and broil,

recipe continues ▸

turning them over occasionally, until they are blackened and blistered, 7 to 10 minutes. Transfer to a heatproof bowl, cover, and let cool completely. Scrape off the blackened skin and remove the seeds and ribs. Finely chop the chilies and transfer them to a small bowl. Cut the limes in half and squeeze in the juice. Stir well and set aside at room temperature until ready to serve.

If you have a kitchen torch, you can use it instead of the broiler to blacken the chiles.

2. **Make the soup:** Heat the oil in a large saucepan over medium heat. Chop the onions by halving them lengthwise and removing the skins. Working with one half at a time, place the onion cut side down and, with your palm on top, make a few horizontal cuts almost all the way to the root end. Make 4 or 5 cuts down through the onion lengthwise, then slice crosswise to make small dice. Add the chopped onions to the pot. Cook, stirring occasionally, until the onions are glazed and shiny, about 4 minutes.

3. Peel the potatoes and cut them into ¾-inch (2-cm) pieces. Add the broth and the potatoes to the pot and bring to a boil. Drain the red and white kidney beans and stir them into the soup and return to a boil. Reduce the heat to medium-low.

4. Simmer, uncovered, until the potatoes are nice and soft, about 30 minutes. Season to taste with salt and pepper.

5. Coarsely chop the cilantro leaves, including some of the tender stems. Put the cilantro in a small bowl. Cut the limes into quarters. Ladle the soup into bowls and serve with the cilantro, limes, and salsa so everyone can season the soup as they wish.

WARM POTATOES
WITH GREENS AND HERBS

SERVES 6

I call this a potato salad, but truthfully, the potatoes are so outnumbered by greens, fresh herbs, and crunchy peas that the name doesn't really do it justice. You'll find simple vegetarian entrées like this one on our family dinner table all year long. Because this is served warm, this dish is equally welcome in the colder months as well as summer. The dish becomes very creamy without a lot of mayonnaise because the potatoes break down a bit when you stir them, adding their starch to the sauce. This is great as is, but if you add bits of fried bacon, shreds of smoked salmon, or even a big spoonful of fish roe or caviar, it's fantastic. If you have lovage or chervil growing in the garden, it will go very nicely in this dish. Serve this with slices of toasted dark bread.

MAYONNAISE

Large egg yolk	1
Dijon mustard	1 teaspoon
Grainy Dijon mustard	1 teaspoon
Canola oil	½ cup (120 ml)
Fine sea salt	
Freshly ground black pepper	

Yukon Gold potatoes	1¼ pounds (570 g)
Fresh peas in the pod	1 pound (455 g) (or 1 cup frozen peas)
Fresh leaf spinach	3 ounces (85 g), about ½ bunch
Lacinato (Tuscan) kale	4 leaves
Salted butter	2 tablespoons
Fresh dill sprigs	25
Fresh parsley sprigs	20
Fresh basil sprigs	20
Fresh cilantro sprigs	20
Lemon	1
Fine sea salt	
Freshly ground black pepper	

recipe continues ▸

1. **Make the mayonnaise:** Whisk the egg yolks, Dijon mustard, and grainy mustard in a medium bowl until combined. About 1 teaspoon at a time, drizzle in the oil, whisking until you have a nice thick mayo. This should take a couple of minutes, so don't rush it. Season with salt and pepper to taste.

2. Scrub the potatoes under cold running water, and put them in a medium saucepan with enough water to cover. Bring to a boil over high heat. Reduce the heat to medium and simmer until the potatoes are tender when pierced with the tip of a knife, about 20 minutes.

3. While the potatoes are cooking, prepare the other ingredients. Shell the fresh peas, if using, into a bowl. If using frozen, put them in a small bowl and cover with cold water to thaw. Strip and discard the thick stems from the spinach and rinse the leaves well. Strip the kale off the tough center stems.

4. Bring a saucepan of water to a boil. Add the butter and when it melts add the fresh peas. They almost instantly change color to a richer brighter green. When that happens, use a wire skimmer or a sieve to scoop them into a bowl. Leave the water boiling.

5. Stir in the kale and let it cook just until it turns a deeper shade of green, about 10 seconds. Using the skimmer, transfer the kale to a colander to drain. Repeat with the spinach. Pat the greens dry on paper towels.

6. Drain the potatoes and return them to their cooking pot to keep warm.

7. Coarsely chop the dill, parsley, basil, and cilantro leaves (you can include some of their tender stems, but discard the thick ones). Squeeze the greens well to press out any excess liquid, and chop them, too.

8. Add the chopped herbs, peas, and greens to the potatoes. Gradually stir in as much of the mayonnaise as you like (it should only be a thin glaze), using a wooden spoon to mix it around. Some of the potatoes will break up and fall apart and that's what you want. Finely grate the lemon zest over the salad. Cut the lemon in half and squeeze in the juice. Mix again. Season with salt and pepper. Transfer to a serving bowl and serve warm.

PORRIDGE WITH WILD MUSHROOMS AND EGGS

MAKES 2 SERVINGS

In Denmark there is an old tradition of ending a meal with a portion of plain boiled grains, a throwback to times when meat was scarce and grains provided an economical way to fill empty bellies. The practice is less common now, but for a hectic day it's still a quick way to make an easy hot and filling dish in about 10 minutes. Pull together whatever toppings you like—bits of bacon or ham, chopped fresh herbs, or leftover greens to supplement the eggs— while the cooked oats rest. It's a comforting dish when you're starting to feel sick or run down.

Whole milk	2 cups (480 ml)
Old-fashioned oats	1½ cups (150 grams)
Wild mushrooms	5 ounces (140 g), such as porcini, chanterelles, or shiitake
Grapeseed or canola oil	2 tablespoons
Fine sea salt	
Freshly ground black pepper	
Large eggs	2
Salted butter	2 tablespoons

1. Stir the milk and oats together in a medium saucepan. Cook over medium heat, stirring constantly to prevent scorching, until the mixture comes to a full boil. Remove from the heat, cover tightly, and set aside.

2. Rinse the mushrooms quickly under cold running water, but don't soak them. Pat the mushrooms dry and slice them thinly.

   I store whole mushrooms uncovered on paper towels in the fridge to dry them out a bit; they cook up drier that way. It's okay if they start to shrivel a tiny bit.

3. Heat 1 tablespoon of the oil in a medium nonstick skillet over medium-high heat. Add the mushrooms and let them cook without stirring until they begin

recipe continues ▶

to brown and crisp, about 3 minutes. Give them a stir and cook just until tender, about 2 minutes, stirring frequently. Season to taste with salt and pepper.

4. Quickly rinse and dry the skillet. Reheat the pan over medium heat. Add the remaining 1 tablespoon oil and heat it until hot but not smoking. Crack the eggs into the pan and cook until the whites are mostly set and the edges are crisp, about 1 minute. Add the butter to the pan and let it melt. Using a long-handled spoon, baste the eggs with the melted butter until the yolk is covered with a thin white film, about 1 minute more. Remove from the heat.

    Hold the eggs just an inch or so above the skillet when you crack them to reduce the chance of the yolk breaking.

5. Stir the oatmeal well and divide it between 2 large bowls. Top each serving with an egg and some mushrooms. Serve immediately.

CONGRATULATIONS: YOU CAN MAKE CHICKEN BROTH

I don't think you can ever have too much broth. Keep a jar in the fridge and try these variations:

- Add some vegetables, such as carrots, celery, leeks, or onion, with the carcass. Herbs (such as rosemary or thyme) are also good.
- Give the broth an Asian flavor with a chopped stalk of lemongrass.
- Use homemade broth to improve your risotto and soups.
- Feeling a little weak? Serve this broth as you would tea, piping hot, with a little freshly squeezed lemon juice.
- Add other fresh vegetables to the soup just before serving. Try shredded fresh spinach leaves or sliced cooked asparagus.

GINGERED CHICKEN BROTH
WITH FENNEL AND SOY EGG

SERVES 2 OR 3

As far back as I can remember, roast chicken (page 195) has been one of my absolute favorite things to eat, and one reason is all the great things you can do with the leftovers. I never throw away the carcass, which is perfect for making broth. Rather than store it in the freezer I've gotten in the habit of making a simple broth the same night I serve the chicken, letting it simmer while I clean up the kitchen. That way, I have a jump on the next day's dinner (or breakfast!) and can make use of every last little bit of flavor from the roasting pan. There's nothing more comforting than a hot bowl of this broth with some fresh vegetables and a savory soy egg, and you can make it more substantial by adding ramen noodles or cooked grains, bits of the chicken you saved from the carcass, or really, just about anything.

BROTH

Roasted chicken carcass	1
Boiling water	2 cups (480 ml)
Garlic	1 head
Fresh ginger	1 (1-inch/2.5-cm) piece
Leek	1
Soy sauce	

SOY EGGS

Fine sea salt	
Large eggs	2
Soy sauce	1 tablespoon, or as needed
Fennel	Stalks and fronds from 1 bulb, or ¼ small bulb
Fresh cilantro leaves	20
Fresh chives	10

1. **To make the broth:** Pick off as much meat as possible from the carcass and save for another use. Break the carcass apart and put it in a medium saucepan

recipe continues ▸

with any bits of skin. Pour the boiling water into the roasting pan the chicken cooked in and use a wooden spatula to loosen as much of the tasty brown drippings as possible. Empty the mixture into the saucepan and add 1 quart (960 ml) cold water, or enough to cover the bones.

2. Rub off the garlic's papery outer husk. Thinly slice the unpeeled ginger. Coarsely chop the white and pale green parts of the leek and rinse well in a colander under cold running water to remove all of the grit. Add the leek, garlic, and ginger and bring to a boil over medium heat. Reduce the heat to very low. Simmer the broth, uncovered, for about 2 hours, or until the liquid has reduced by about half.

   I normally just turn the heat off after about 2 hours, by which point the liquid has reduced quite a bit. I leave the pot overnight in a cool part of the kitchen or even outdoors, then refrigerate it the next morning. If the weather is warm, you can put the pot in a sink of ice water and let the broth cool down until tepid, then refrigerate it, uncovered, overnight.

3. When you are ready to serve, strain the broth through a fine-mesh sieve into another pot, discarding the solids. Return the broth to a full boil and cook until it reduces a bit more and the flavor is nice and strong, about 5 minutes. Season to taste with soy sauce.

4. **While the broth cooks down, make the soy eggs:** Bring a small saucepan of water to a boil. When the water boils, add 1 teaspoon or so of salt. Use a slotted spoon to lower the eggs into the water. Reduce the heat to medium. Cook the eggs for 5 minutes. Turn off the heat and let the eggs stand in the water for 2 minutes. Place the saucepan in the sink and run cold water into the pan until the water feels cool.

   If you have a timer, use it when you cook the eggs. An extra minute makes a difference.

5. As soon as the eggs are cool enough to handle, peel them and place them in a small bowl. Pour the soy sauce over the eggs and set aside for 5 minutes, turning and swirling them to get a nice, even brown color all over.

6. Thinly slice the fennel stalks and fronds, or the bulb if using. Coarsely chop the cilantro and finely chop the chives. Divide the fennel, cilantro, and chives between 2 soup bowls.

7. To serve, ladle the hot broth into the bowls, which will lightly cook the fennel and release the flavor of the herbs. Place an egg in each bowl. Serve hot, with soy sauce on the side.

SAVORY SWEET POTATO TART

SERVES 6

Dishes like this one are a good example of why it's always a good idea to roast a few extras whenever you make sweet potatoes. When I serve this, the kids feel like they are getting away with having cake for dinner; even though it's not sweet at all, it does look like a special, fancy confection. The play of textures is really appealing, with the smooth potato custard sandwiched inside a crunchy pastry shell and the crispy potato crust on top. It's a soothing main dish that doesn't need much more than a green salad. You can roast the potatoes and prebake the tart shell up to a day ahead of time to make this a relatively easy weeknight dinner.

Sweet potatoes	2 small (about 1 pound/455 g)

TART DOUGH

Cold salted butter	½ cup (110 g)
Unbleached all-purpose flour	1½ cups (210 g)
Fine sea salt	⅛ teaspoon
Ice water	3 tablespoons, as needed
Large eggs, lightly beaten	2
Parmigiano-Reggiano cheese	1 cup (110 g) freshly grated, plus 2 tablespoons
Fine sea salt	
Freshly ground black pepper	
Yukon Gold potatoes	3 medium (about 12 ounces/340 g)
Extra-virgin olive oil	1 teaspoon, plus more for serving

1. **Bake the sweet potatoes:** Preheat the oven to 400°F (200°C). Scrub the sweet potatoes but leave them unpeeled. Pierce each one a few times with a fork and place them on a small, rimmed baking sheet. Bake until tender when pierced with a small. sharp knife, about 1 hour. Split them open to release the steam and let cool until lukewarm.

   If the sweet potatoes are too hot, they could curdle the eggs in the filling; if too cold, they won't mash to a smooth purée.

recipe continues ▸

2. **Make the tart dough:** Cut the butter into small cubes. Put the flour and salt in a medium bowl, add the butter, and toss to coat the butter. Using your fingertips, rub the butter into the flour—the mixture will look like coarse crumbs with some larger flakes.

   You can also pulse the flour and butter together in a food processor until the mixture looks like coarse crumbs with pea-sized bits of butter, then transfer the mixture to a bowl.

3. Stirring with a fork, sprinkle in the water just until the mixture clumps together and can be gathered up into a ball. It should feel something like modeling clay, but not wet. If it's too dry, mix in more ice water by the half-teaspoon.

4. Lightly butter a 9-inch (23-cm) tart pan with a removable bottom. Break up the dough into walnut-sized chunks, and with your fingers press it onto the bottom and up the sides of the pan, making sure it isn't too thick where the bottom meets the sides. It should protrude about ⅛ inch (3 mm) above the rim of the pan. Keep pressing and spreading the bits of dough with your fingers to join them together and line the pan as evenly as possible. Refrigerate the tart shell for 15 minutes.

5. Preheat the oven to 375°F (190°C).

6. Pierce the dough all over with a fork. Place the pan on a baking sheet. Line the bottom and sides of the dough with a large piece of parchment paper and fill it about halfway with dried beans.

   Weighting the crust will help keep the sides of your tart shell from slipping down as it bakes. You can reuse the beans for baking; just cool them before storing in a jar or plastic bag.

7. Bake until the visible edges of the dough look drier and set, about 15 minutes. Remove the pan on the sheet from the oven. Lift off the parchment paper with the beans and set them aside. Return the baking sheet and pan to the oven and bake until the crust is barely browned, 7 to 10 minutes. Remove from the oven and let cool for 5 to 10 minutes. Keep the oven on.

8. **Make the filling:** Split the sweet potatoes and scoop the flesh into a medium bowl. Mash the sweet potatoes well. Mix in the eggs a bit at a time. Add the 1 cup (110 g) Parmigiano, ¼ teaspoon salt, and ⅛ teaspoon pepper and mix again.

recipe continues ▸

9. Scrub the Yukon Gold potatoes but leave them unpeeled. Pat them dry. Use a mandoline or V-slicer to thinly slice the potatoes into rounds about ⅓ inch (8 mm) thick. Spread the sweet potato filling in the crust. Top with overlapping rows of potatoes arranged in circles. You may have leftover potatoes. Drizzle with the oil and season lightly with salt. Sprinkle with the remaining 2 tablespoons Parmigiano.

10. Bake until the potato crust is tender and beginning to brown, about 40 minutes. (If you want to brown the potatoes more, raise the oven temperature to 425°F/220°C and bake for another few minutes.)

11. Let the tart cool in the pan for 10 minutes. Remove the sides of the pan, cut the tart into wedges, and serve warm with a fruity olive oil to drizzle over each serving.

CONGRATULATIONS: YOU CAN MAKE A SAVORY TART

Because this dough doesn't have any sugar, it is perfect for both savory and sweet fillings. I use the same dough to make the Apricot Tart with Frangipane on page 235. Savory tarts and quiches are an easy one-dish meal that is also good for using up odds and ends when you haven't had time to shop. All you need is a few eggs to bind the filling and a green salad on the side. Half-fill the par-baked tart shell with chopped cooked meats (ham, sausage, bacon, or even flaked salmon or crabmeat) and cooked vegetables (such as blanched asparagus, sautéed zucchini, or squeezed-out spinach). Sprinkle with ½ cup (55 g) shredded cheese (Gruyère, Comté, Swiss, or Cheddar), and 1 tablespoon minced fresh chives or tarragon, if you wish. Whisk together 1 cup (240 ml) half-and-half and 2 large eggs, then season with salt and freshly ground black pepper. Pour in as much of the custard as needed. Bake in a preheated 350°F (180°C) oven until the filling is puffed and golden, about 30 minutes. Let cool for 10 minutes before removing the sides of the pan and serving.

KALE AND MUSHROOM "CARBONARA"

SERVES 2 TO 3

When René has spent a long day working out new dishes in the test kitchen at Noma, he often comes home feeling ready for something on the healthy side and usually vegetarian. On one such night, he threw this eggy vegetable dish together in just a few minutes, and now it has become a weeknight mainstay. You could treat many other vegetables in the same way, but the earthy mixture of mushrooms and sturdy kale is particularly filling. Meaty portobello mushrooms work really well here, but you can use any kind of wild or cultivated mushrooms or a mixture; you'll get more different textures that way. This is also a wonderful side dish with roast ribs or chicken, or pan-fried fish.

Portobello mushroom caps	2
Kale	1 pound (455 g)
Extra-virgin olive oil	⅓ cup (75 ml)
Chicken broth	⅓ cup (75 ml)
Ground ancho, chipotle, or Aleppo chile	2 teaspoons
Large egg yolks	4
Parmigiano-Reggiano cheese	1 cup (110 g), freshly grated
Flaky sea salt	
Freshly ground black pepper	

1. Preheat the oven to 325°F (165°C).

2. Wipe the mushrooms clean with a moist tea towel. Place them on a rimmed baking sheet. Bake the mushrooms just until they are warmed, without browning, 6 to 8 minutes. This will give them a meatier texture. Remove them from the oven, let cool slightly, and cut into thin strips.

3. While the mushrooms are roasting, wash the kale well under cold running water. Spin the kale dry in a salad spinner. (Or lay the leaves on tea towels, place more towels on top, and roll them up to soak up the water.) The kale

recipe continues ▸

should be as dry as possible. Strip off and discard the tough stems from the kale. Tear the leaves into bite-sized pieces.

Be extra diligent when washing the kale, because if it is sandy, it will ruin the whole dish.

4. Heat a large saucepan over medium-high heat. Add the oil and heat until it is hot but not smoking. Add the kale and cook without stirring until the pieces at the bottom of the pot turn a shade darker, about 30 seconds. Stir in the mushrooms and cook, stirring constantly, 30 seconds more. Add the broth and cook until it has reduced to a glaze, 4 to 5 minutes.

5. Remove from the heat and stir in the ground chile. Let cool for a few minutes.

6. Using a fork, mix the egg yolks and Parmigiano in a small bowl and set the mixture aside.

Don't use a whisk for this—the cheese tends to stick to the wires.

7. Gradually add the egg mixture to the greens, using kitchen tongs to toss them together so the eggs coat the vegetables nicely. Keep the egg mixture moving, especially on the bottom of the saucepan—you don't want it to set and turn into scrambled eggs.

8. Season with salt and pepper. Dish this up straight from the pot, or divide among bowls and serve immediately.

CHEESE RAVIOLI
WITH BROWN-BUTTER EGG YOLKS,
PARMESAN, AND SAGE

SERVES 4

*For a pantry meal, this has a lot of plate appeal. You can trace its roots back
to a dish that was served at Noma featuring an egg yolk cured in beef juice. I found I
could approximate the creamy, unctuous quality in a way that was more practical
for a home kitchen by bathing the yolk in brown butter. I got the idea of pairing
the yolk with ravioli one night when we had unexpected dinner guests and not a
lot in the fridge. Fortunately, the combination turned out to be fantastic, and
if you have good-quality cheese ravioli in the freezer (get the oversized ones
if possible), this comes together quickly in a rather impressive way. It's quite rich,
so I serve it as an entrée rather than a starter, with just a simple salad.*

Large egg yolks	4
Salted butter	¾ cup (1½ sticks; 165 grams)
Coarse sea salt	
Large cheese ravioli	16
Fresh sage sprigs	2 or 3
Extra-virgin olive oil	For serving
Parmigiano-Reggiano cheese	1 (6-ounce/170-g) chunk

1. Separate the eggs, dropping each yolk into its own small bowl. Cut the butter
   into tablespoons and place in a medium saucepan. Melt the butter over
   medium heat until foamy. Continue cooking, whisking constantly, until the
   butter smells nutty and the milk solids at the bottom turn light brown, 2 to
   3 minutes. Immediately remove the brown butter from the heat. Carefully
   divide the butter among the 4 bowls, pouring it down the sides of the bowl,
   to cover the yolks entirely. Set aside for about 20 minutes.

   Do not pour the butter directly onto the fragile yolks or they may break.

recipe continues ▶

2. Bring a large pot of water to boil. Add a tablespoon or so of salt. Add the ravioli and cook according to the package directions until they float to the top of the water and are tender. Cut the sage leaves into thin shreds.

3. Drain the ravioli well and arrange 4 on each plate. Gently slip an egg yolk onto the center of each portion and drizzle the brown butter over all. Sprinkle with the basil and sage. Grate as much Parmigiano as you like on top. Serve immediately, offering olive oil at the table for drizzling.

CONGRATULATIONS: YOU CAN MAKE BROWN BUTTER

Brown butter will keep, tightly covered in the fridge, for about a week, so if you are making some for this sauce, it's easy to make a double batch and store half in a glass jar. The brown sediment will settle to the bottom of the jar, so before you use it, let it come to room temperature, stir to recombine, then:

• Make the roasted celery root on page 201.
• Smear it on a piece of bread.
• Drizzle it onto soup as a garnish.
• Serve it with fried or baked fish.
• Toss it with hot boiled potatoes and chopped dill or other herbs.

You can also cut the chilled brown butter into small cubes and use it to flavor vanilla ice cream, which is spectacular. Add it just before the ice cream is fully frozen, letting the paddle incorporate the bits into the custard.

JAPANESE OMELET
WITH FRIED STICKY RICE

SERVES 4

When we spent summers in France during my childhood, my mother often made an omelet as a simple weeknight meal, and I still find them homey and comforting. Adding a few interesting textural elements, like pickled onions and crisp bits of sticky rice, makes them even better. A few years ago, Noma did a pop-up restaurant in Tokyo, and the whole family spent two months there. During that time, we developed an obsession with sticky rice. This dish is one of the best ways I've found to use cold leftover rice; don't make it with freshly cooked rice, or it won't fry up properly. I make one big, billowy omelet and place it in the center of the table so everyone can dig in with their spoons. A nonstick pan simplifies omelet-making enormously.

PINK ONIONS

Red onion	1 medium
Cider vinegar	1 cup (240 ml), as needed
Sugar	½ teaspoon
Fine sea salt	½ teaspoon

TOMATO AND AVOCADO SALAD

Tomatoes	2 medium
Hass avocados	2
Lemon	1
Extra-virgin olive oil	1 tablespoon
Fine sea salt	
Finely ground black pepper	

OMELET

Canola oil	2 tablespoons
Cold cooked sticky rice	¾ cup (120 g)
Large eggs	8
Whole milk	1 tablespoon
Fine sea salt	

recipe continues ▶

1. **Make the pink onions:** Cut off the top and bottom ends of the onion. Cut the onion in half lengthwise and peel off the skin. One at a time, place an onion half, cut side down, on the work surface and cut into thin half-moons. Mix the vinegar, sugar, and salt in a shallow bowl. Add the onion and mix with your fingers, separating the layers. Add more vinegar to cover the onion, if needed. Set aside while preparing the remaining ingredients.

2. **Make the salad:** To core the tomatoes easily, slice each one downward next to but not through the stem. Make two angled cuts into the large half to release the core and discard. Slice the tomatoes into chunks. Halve and pit the avocados and use the tip of your knife to cut them into thick slices. Use a large spoon to scoop out the slices. Arrange the tomatoes and avocados together on a platter. Halve the lemon and squeeze the juice over the salad. Drizzle with the olive oil and season with the salt and pepper.

   The oil, lemon juice, and tomato juice will keep the avocados from discoloring.

3. **Make the omelet:** Put the oil in a large (10- to 11-inch/25- to 28-cm) nonstick skillet and place over medium heat. When the oil is shimmering but not smoking, use your fingers to crumble the sticky rice, breaking up the clumps (they don't need to be uniform) and carefully drop them into the skillet in a single layer. Cook without stirring for about 2 minutes, or until the rice is nice and golden brown on the bottom.

   Don't pile the rice too deep; you want as much of it as possible to come into contact with the skillet to crisp.

4. While the rice fries, break the eggs into a bowl and give them a quick whisk to combine the yolks and whites. Add the milk and a pinch of salt and whisk again.

5. Reduce the heat to medium. Pour the eggs over the rice and stir with a wooden spatula to combine. Let the eggs cook until they begin to set around the edges, about 45 seconds. Holding the spatula with the bottom parallel to the bottom of the skillet, stir the egg mixture in a circular pattern while shaking the pan back and forth at the same time. The idea is to mix the cooked part on the bottom with the uncooked portion on top. Repeat, letting the eggs cook gently, until they begin to set again, about 30 seconds more. Continue this process every 30 seconds or so until all of the egg mixture is set but still moist on top, about 2 minutes more.

   Shaking the pan while stirring helps the omelet cook evenly and redistributes the uncooked egg.

recipe continues ▸

6. Use the spatula to gently loosen the edge of the omelet nearest the handle, and fold this third of the omelet toward the center. Now, grip the skillet handle from underneath and tilt the pan so the far edge of the omelet begins to slide onto the serving plate. When the omelet is halfway onto the plate, lift the pan perpendicular to the plate so the rest of the omelet folds over onto itself.

It will take a few tries to master making a "perfect" omelet, and the rice does make it a little harder to fold. If it breaks when you roll it onto the plate, don't worry; it will still taste great.

7. Just before serving, lift half of the pickled onions from the vinegar and scatter them over the salad. Serve the omelet with the salad.

Sometimes, the eggs will run a little when you have flipped the omelet onto the plate. This is nothing to be alarmed by, but it doesn't look pretty, so just dab it with a piece of paper towel.

PICKLED ONIONS

Put the remaining onions with their pickling liquid into a small jar or container and refrigerate for up to 1 week. These quick, easy-to-make pickles will become your new best friend, adding crunch, acid, color, and flavor to just about anything you serve:

- Put them on burgers or other sandwiches, such as Marinated Lamb with Pita on page 177.
- Use as a garnish for Duck Breast Rice Bowl on page 129.
- Sprinkle them into any green salad.
- Scatter them over simply grilled or broiled fish.

MONKFISH WITH LEMON SAUCE AND PEAS

SERVES 4

My middle daughter, Genta, calls monkfish "chicken fish" because of its firm, meaty, frankly un-fishlike texture, and it's true that many people who claim not to love fish happily eat this dish. The thin fillets cook quickly and brown beautifully thanks to a hot pan and a last-minute basting with butter, which seals in flavor and makes a delicious crust. When fresh peas are in season, by all means use them—lots of them—but if not, frozen are a fine substitute. This is a great simple dinner on its own, as the peas are both green and starchy, but I might add a salad with some substantial ingredients like red peppers, olives, and feta cheese if I have time. With a good chunk of bread to sop up the buttery lemon sauce (and salad dressing), you're all set.

Peas in the pod	2 pounds (910 g) or 2 cups (300 g) frozen

LEMON SAUCE

Lemons	2
Onion	½ small, halved lengthwise
Dry white vermouth or dry white wine	3 tablespoons
Salted butter	8 tablespoons (110 g)
Fine sea salt	

Monkfish fillet	1½ pounds (680 g) cut into 3-ounce (85-g) portions
Grapeseed or canola oil	3 tablespoons
Cold salted butter	5 tablespoons (70 g)
Fresh thyme sprigs	2

1. If using fresh peas, shuck them into a bowl. If using frozen, place in a bowl and cover with cool water to thaw them. Let them stand for 10 to 15 minutes and drain just before cooking.

   Don't be tempted to cook the peas too early; they can go from sweet and tender to drab and mushy in minutes.

2. **Make the sauce:** Squeeze the lemon juice into a small bowl and strain to remove the seeds. You should have about 6 tablespoons (90 ml).

recipe continues ▸

3. Chop the onion and add to a small saucepan. Add the lemon juice and vermouth and bring to a boil over high heat. Boil until the liquid has reduced to about 2 tablespoons, 3 to 5 minutes. Cut the butter into slices.

4. Reduce the heat to very low. One slice at a time, add the butter and whisk it until it is incorporated but not melted. Continue whisking in the butter, occasionally moving the pan off the heat so the pan can cool slightly, until it has all been incorporated and the sauce is smooth. (Once you get the hang of it, you can add more butter at a time.) Set the sauce aside.

   Don't let the sauce get too hot or it will curdle. Keep moving the pan off the heat to cool it down. It doesn't need to stay piping hot; it will warm up when it hits the hot food.

5. Bring 1 quart (960 ml) water to a boil in a medium saucepan.

6. While the water heats, place a large, dry skillet over high heat. Pat the fish fillets very dry with paper towels. Add the oil and let it heat until it is very hot but not smoking.

   Making sure the fish is very dry helps give it a thin, tasty crust.

7. Add the fish to the skillet and cook without moving it until the bottom is golden brown, about 90 seconds. Using rubber-tipped tongs or a metal spatula, turn the fillets and cook until the second side is golden brown, about 90 seconds more. Turn the fish one more time and add 3 tablespoons of the butter and the thyme to the pan. When the butter has melted, tilt the pan to one side to pool the butter. Using a long-handled metal spoon, baste the fish 6 to 8 times with the melted butter. Transfer the fish to a platter.

   Be patient! When the fish is ready to turn it will release from the pan on its own; don't try to turn it before then, or the fillets will break.

8. Add the remaining 2 tablespoons of butter to the boiling water and, when it melts, add the peas. Cook the peas until they are almost tender and a rich, dark shade of green, 2 to 3 minutes. (Cook thawed peas for 2 minutes only.) Drain the peas and season them with salt.

9. Put the sauce in a serving bowl (you can strain out the onion, if you wish). Serve the fish and peas with the lemon sauce on the side.

FLANK STEAK WITH OVEN-FRIED GARLIC POTATOES AND HERBED PAN SAUCE

MAKES 4 SERVINGS

Most any French bistro can turn out an order of steak frites so reliably good that for years I rarely made it at home because I could never match the juicy perfection of restaurant-made steak. Now, I have learned the secret to getting a steakhouse-style crust on pan-seared meat: basting in butter. The first time I saw a chef spooning hot butter over a steak was in the middle of dinner service at Noma, and I immediately asked the cook "What are you doing?" He was too busy to explain at the moment, but later he told me this is what takes a restaurant steak that extra 10 percent further in developing flavor. Now I use this technique with meat, fish (page 165), and even vegetables (page 62). You can also add a bit of garlic to the butter to coat the meat with even more flavor.

GARLIC OVEN-FRIED POTATOES

Yukon Gold potatoes	4 large
Canola oil	3 tablespoons, as needed
Garlic cloves	2

STEAK

Canola oil	1 tablespoon
Flank steak	1 (1½ pounds/680 g)
Garlic cloves	5
Salted butter	¼ cup (55 g)
Fresh flat-leaf parsley leaves	20
Chicken broth	¼ cup (60 ml)
Flaky sea salt	
Freshly ground black pepper	

1. Preheat the oven to 425°F (220°C).

2. Scrub the potatoes under cold running water and pat them dry. Cut the potatoes lengthwise into ½-inch (12-mm) wedges. Put them on a large,

recipe continues ▸

rimmed baking sheet. Drizzle with 1 tablespoon of the oil and toss to coat. Spread the potatoes, flat side down, in a single layer. Bake until the potatoes can be easily scraped from the sheet with a metal spatula, about 25 minutes. Crush the garlic cloves under the flat side of a knife, but do not peel them. Turn the potatoes and add the garlic. Continue baking until the potatoes are golden brown and tender, about 15 minutes.

3. **To cook the steak:** Place a large skillet over medium-high heat. Let the pan get super hot—it should be just beginning to smoke. While the pan heats, use paper towels to pat the beef dry. Add the oil and tilt to coat the bottom of the skillet. Add the steak and 5 whole garlic cloves. Cook until the underside of the steak is nicely browned, about 4 minutes. Turn and cook the second side for 4 minutes more.

   Get the steak as dry as you can before it goes in the pan. That's what helps get a good sear.

4. When the steak is well seared on both sides, about 8 minutes total, add the butter to the pan and let it melt. Tilt the pan so the butter pools to one side. Add the thyme sprigs. Use a long-handled spoon to baste the meat with the herbed butter for 1 minute. Turn the steak and baste 1 minute more. Transfer the steak and thyme sprigs to a cutting board and let it rest for 3 to 5 minutes, reserving the butter in the pan.

   Cook flank steak no more than medium-rare, or it will be tough.

5. Return the skillet with the melted butter to medium-high heat. Coarsely chop the parsley. Add the broth and bring to a boil, scraping up the browned bits in the bottom of the skillet with a wooden spoon. Cook, stirring constantly, until the sauce is slightly reduced, about 30 seconds. Stir in the parsley and season to taste with salt and pepper. Pour into a small serving bowl.

6. Cut the steak across the grain into thin slices and arrange on a warm platter. Scoop the potatoes into a serving bowl. Season the steak and potatoes with salt and pepper and serve with the sauce.

CONGRATULATIONS: YOU CAN COOK STEAK LIKE A STEAKHOUSE VET

The same sear-and-baste method as above will work with almost any cut of steak you like (such as strip steak, rib eye, or sirloin), but depending on the cut and thickness, you may have to adjust the cooking time a bit. The average is 4 minutes per side for steaks cut 1 inch (2.5 cm) thick. Hanger steak is a similarly flavorful, chewy cut, but the steaks are a bit plumper and will need an extra 1 to 2 minutes on each side, while thin skirt steaks will cook even more quickly than flank.

PORTUGUESE PORK CHOPS AND RICE

SERVES 2

As a child in Portugal, I always came running when my mother made this, and the smell of the pork, garlic, and lemon cooking together still makes me hungry immediately. I actually prefer pork to steak. It's meaty but lighter, and I don't need to eat a lot to be satisfied. Cooking the garlic cloves in the skin protects them from burning. If you have some chopped fresh herbs (thyme, rosemary, chives, and cilantro are all good), sprinkle them over the chops and rice just before serving. And don't skip the rice; it's just too good with a drizzle of the pan sauce.

Center-cut loin pork chops	2 (12 ounces/340 g), cut 1½ inches (4 cm) thick
Basmati or sticky rice	½ cup (100 g)
Fine sea salt	
Lemon	1
Canola oil	1 tablespoon
Garlic cloves	6 small
Salted butter	3 tablespoons

1. Take the pork chops out of the fridge 1 hour before you cook them.

2. **About 30 minutes before you plan to eat, start the rice:** Bring 1 cup (240 ml) water and the rice to a boil over medium-high heat in a medium saucepan. Stir once, but do not stir again! Reduce the heat to low and cover tightly. Cook until the water is absorbed and little air pockets appear on the top of the rice, about 15 minutes. Remove from the heat and let stand, covered, for 10 minutes.

   Don't stir the rice once it is simmering, as that will make it sticky and lumpy.

3. Once the rice is simmering, heat a large skillet over medium-high heat. Pat the pork chops on both sides with paper towels to get them as dry as possible. Season the pork with salt.

recipe continues ▸

4. Cut the lemon into 8 to 10 wedges and set them aside. When the pan is very hot, add the oil and heat until shimmering but not smoking. Add the pork chops and cook without moving them until browned on the underside, about 3 minutes. Turn the chops and scatter the lemon wedges and the unpeeled garlic in the pan. Cook the chops until browned on the second side, about 3 minutes more.

   Don't turn the chops until there is a mixture of dark caramel and golden brown colors on the bottom. This step is where the flavor develops.

5. Now, add the butter to the skillet and let it melt. Tilting the skillet to pool the melted butter, use a long-handled spoon to baste the chops almost continuously for about 2 minutes. Turn the chops one last time and baste 1 minute longer.

   Basting the chops with butter will give them flavor, but it also helps make them juicier by adding moisture to the skillet.

6. Transfer the chops and lemon wedges to a platter and let the chops rest for 3 to 5 minutes. Season the chops with salt. While they rest, add about ½ cup (120 ml) water to the garlic cloves and pan juices in the skillet and stir over medium heat, scraping up any browned bits from the bottom of the pan with a wooden spatula. Cook the sauce until slightly reduced, about 1 minute. Remove from the heat.

7. When the chops have rested, slice the meat off the bone in one large piece. Slice the meat crosswise and serve with the rice, pouring the pan sauce over all.

MIDDLE EASTERN BEEF WITH LENTILS

SERVES 4

My family doesn't eat meat every day, and when we do we don't necessarily have enormous portions, so small bites of beef need to have a ton of great flavor. Marinating builds in more flavor notes, especially in meat that doesn't cook very long. I often put meat to marinate in the fridge before I leave the house in the morning; when we are ready for dinner, I cook it quickly over high heat, just long enough to fry the spices without burning them. Cooking lentils slowly as you would risotto keeps them more separate, with a toothier texture. It's another example of taking a humble ingredient and preparing it with the care you would use for a more valuable commodity.

MARINATED BEEF

Boneless beef sirloin steak	1½ pounds (680 g), cut 1 inch (2.5 cm) thick
Garlic cloves	6
Coriander seeds	2 teaspoons
Fennel seeds	2 teaspoons
Extra-virgin olive oil	½ cup (120 ml)
Sweet paprika	2 teaspoons
Fresh thyme sprigs	5

LENTILS

Canola oil	2 teaspoons
Onion	1
Puy (green) lentils	1 cup (200 g)
Bay leaves	2
Dry white wine	1 cup (240 ml)
Chicken broth	5 cups (1.2 L), as needed
Fine sea salt	
Freshly ground black pepper	
Tomatoes	3 medium
Flaky salt	
Fresh cilantro leaves	30

recipe continues ▸

1. **Marinate the beef:** Cut the beef into ½-inch (12-mm) strips. Crush the garlic cloves with the flat side of your knife and discard the papery skins. Use a mortar and pestle or a spice mill to grind the coriander and fennel seeds to a powder. Add the garlic, coriander, and fennel to a large bowl. Add the oil, paprika, and thyme and mix well. Add the beef and massage the marinade into the meat. Cover and refrigerate for up to 24 hours.

   If you don't have a spice mill, use a coffee grinder. Whir a bit of rice in the grinder before and after grinding the spices to clean it.

2. **To make the lentils:** Heat the oil in a medium saucepan over medium heat. Chop the onion and add it to the saucepan. Cook without stirring until it is lightly browned on the bottom, about 2 minutes. Stir the onion and continue to cook until it is golden brown, about 3 minutes more.

3. Add the lentils and bay leaves and stir for 1 minute. Turn the heat down to low and stir in the wine. Let the wine simmer until only about 1 tablespoon remains. Stir in about 2 cups (480 ml) of the broth to just barely cover the lentils, and bring to a boil over high heat. Reduce the heat to medium-low and cover. Simmer the lentils, stirring every 5 to 7 minutes and adding more broth in ½-cup (120-ml) increments as needed to keep the lentils covered. After 15 minutes, taste a lentil or two before you add more broth, and stop adding broth when they still have a bit of snap, about 20 minutes. Season to taste with the salt and pepper.

4. Coarsely chop the tomatoes. Add them to the lentils, but don't stir them in. Cover the saucepan and remove from the heat.

5. **Now, to cook the beef:** Heat a large skillet over medium-high heat. When the pan is very hot, add half of the meat in a single layer. Cook the meat without moving it for 30 seconds, then use tongs to turn each piece. Cook on the second side for about 1½ minutes, then turn again. Cook for a final 30 seconds and transfer to a bowl. Quickly reheat the skillet, and cook the remaining beef the same way. Season the meat strips with the salt. Chop half of the cilantro leaves and stir them into the beef.

   You will not need to add oil to the skillet because of the marinade clinging to the beef.

6. Give the lentils a quick stir to mix in the tomatoes. Spoon the lentils into serving bowls. Top with the beef, sprinkle with the reserved cilantro, and serve.

MARINATED LAMB WITH PITA AND HUMMUS

SERVES 6

Back when I was the only one of my girlfriends who had kids, we met at my house once a week for dinner, and I usually did the cooking. One of my friends requested pita sandwiches and I was horrified, thinking of the sad, bland fare you get in a cafeteria where they come stuffed with tuna or ham and thousand-island dressing. Gross! My compromise was this kebab-inspired sandwich stuffed with fresh vegetables, well-seasoned lamb, and a dab of hummus instead of the more-expected tzatziki. The marinade really stands up to the gamey lamb and veggies. Buy a boneless leg of lamb roast for this recipe. You won't need it all, so cut the rest into smaller portions to freeze (be sure to label them!) for future meals.

MARINATED LAMB

Boneless leg of lamb	1¼ pounds (570 g)
Garlic cloves	6
Extra-virgin olive oil	½ cup (120 ml)
Fresh rosemary sprigs	5
Garam masala	⅓ cup (30 g)
Smoked paprika	2 teaspoons

HUMMUS

Chickpeas	1 (15-ounce/420-g) can
Tahini	2 tablespoons
Extra-virgin olive oil	2 tablespoons, plus more for drizzling
Fresh lemon juice	1 tablespoon
Fine sea salt	

Tomatoes	2
Fine sea salt	
Extra-virgin olive oil	
Cucumber	1
Plain Greek yogurt	½ cup (120 ml)
Whole-wheat pita breads	6
Fresh flat-leaf parsley	30 leaves
Smoked paprika	For garnish

recipe continues ▸

1. **To marinate the lamb:** At least 2 hours (or up to 1 day) before cooking, cut the lamb into strips about ½ inch (12 mm) wide and 1½ inches (4 cm) long. Crush the garlic cloves under the flat side of a knife and peel the garlic. Put the garlic, oil, rosemary, garam masala, and smoked paprika in a glass, ceramic, or metal bowl. Add the meat and mix well so that all the meat is covered in the marinade. Cover and refrigerate for at least 2 hours.

   Don't use a plastic container for this unless you don't mind if the spices stain it.

2. **Make the hummus:** Drain the chickpeas. Add them to a food processor or blender along with the tahini, the 2 tablespoons oil, and the lemon juice and process until smooth. Season to taste with salt. Transfer to a serving bowl and drizzle with a little more olive oil.

3. To core the tomatoes easily, slice each downward next to but not through the stem. Make two angled cuts into the larger half to release the core and discard. Slice the tomato lengthwise into thin wedges. Put in a serving bowl, sprinkle with a little salt, and drizzle with olive oil.

4. Peel the cucumber, cut it in half lengthwise, then into thin slices, and transfer to a serving bowl. Put the yogurt in a small serving bowl.

5. Preheat the oven to 350°F (180°C).

6. Warm the pitas by placing them right on the oven rack for about 5 minutes. Wrap them in a tea towel to keep warm.

7. **Now, for the lamb:** Drain the meat in a colander to remove the excess oil. Discard the rosemary and garlic. Heat a large skillet over medium-high heat. When it is very hot, add half of the meat strips. Cook the meat without moving it for 30 seconds, then turn the pieces and cook on the second side for about 1½ minutes more. Turn the pieces one last time and cook for a final 30 seconds—the lamb should be nicely browned. Transfer the meat to a bowl. Reheat the skillet and repeat with the remaining meat strips. Don't put too much meat in the pan at once, or it will give off too much steam and boil rather than brown. You won't need any oil in the skillet because of the oil in the marinade. Chop half of the parsley and stir it into the lamb mixture.

8. Put the remaining parsley in a small bowl. Arrange the lamb, vegetables, hummus, yogurt, and parsley on a platter and serve with the pitas.

GYOZA

SERVES 4 TO 6; MAKES ABOUT 44

Some may think of gyoza as an appetizer, but for me, three is never enough, and we often make a meal of these crisply fried dumplings, rice, and a salad. I became completely obsessed with gyoza after spending some time in Japan and got in the habit of keeping a bag of frozen dumplings in the freezer. But I was never entirely comfortable about what might be in the filling, and I didn't feel the frozen ones cooked up as well, either. Luckily, with pre-made wrappers these are very fast to make. Filling and folding the dumplings is a great communal activity, and the kids love to help. Our oldest, Arwen, pleats the skins like a pro, while Genta's tend to be a bit more freeform, but they all taste good. This recipe may seem like it makes a lot, but I have never had any leftovers; we just keep eating until they are gone.

DIPPING SAUCE

Fresh ginger	1 (1-inch/2.5-cm) piece
Soy sauce	⅔ cup (165 ml)
Garlic clove	1
Toasted sesame oil	2 tablespoons
Chile oil	2 teaspoons
Finely sliced fresh chives	2 teaspoons

GYOZA

Scallions	2
Garlic cloves	3
Pork sausage	1 pound (455 g)
Fine sea salt	1 teaspoon
Cornstarch	1 tablespoon, for sprinkling
Round Asian dumpling wrappers	1 pound (455 g), about 44
Peanut or canola oil	2 tablespoons, as needed

1. **Make the sauce:** Peel the ginger or shred it on the large holes of a box grater. Combine the ginger and soy sauce in a small bowl. Using a garlic press,

recipe continues ▸

crush the garlic into the bowl. Add the sesame oil, chile oil, and chives and stir to combine.

Use the tip of a teaspoon to scrape the skin off the ginger.

2. **Make the gyoza:** Finely chop both the white and green parts of the scallions. Crush the garlic cloves under the flat side of a knife and discard the skins. Remove the sausage from the casings and place in a bowl with the salt, scallions, and garlic and mix well with your hands to distribute the seasonings. Line a rimmed baking sheet with parchment or wax paper and sprinkle with the cornstarch.

3. Place a small bowl of water on your work surface. Place a dumpling wrapper in the palm of your nondominant hand. Spoon about 1 teaspoon of the pork mixture into the center of the wrapper. Dip the first two fingers of your free hand in the water and moisten the edges of the wrapper. Fold the wrapper in half to enclose the filling, and pleat the edges in five tight folds to seal. Place the gyoza, with the pleated edge standing up, on the baking sheet. Repeat with the remaining wrappers and filling.

Do not overstuff the dumplings, as the filling will expand as it cooks.

4. **Cook the gyoza:** Heat the oil in a large, nonstick frying pan over medium-high heat until the oil is shimmering but not smoking. Carefully place the gyoza in the pan, pleated edge up and nestled closely together side by side. Let them cook until golden brown on the bottom, about 1 minute. Add about ½ cup (120 ml) water. Partially cover the pan leaving the lid slightly askew and cook until the water has boiled away and the dumplings are sizzling, 5 to 7 minutes.

If you have a relatively large skillet, you can probably cook all the gyoza at once; otherwise, use two skillets or cook them in two batches.

5. Slide the gyoza onto a plate. Serve hot, with individual small bowls of the sauce for dipping.

BREADED FISH FILLETS
WITH BROCCOLI

SERVES 4

*As a kid, I loved, loved fish sticks, and they were really the only kind of fish I ate—
probably because I couldn't really taste the fish at all under all that heavy breading.
I no longer resort to a package from the freezer for crisply breaded and fried fillets
like these, but my kids love them just as much now as I did then. I've found most
people find a crisply fried fillet or cutlet irresistible. This basic method is a
good introduction to deep-frying, the gateway to a host of dishes like the
Tonkatsu Chicken on page 187 or the super-savory Eggplant Gratin on page 108.*

Broccoli	1 head
Skinless fish fillets	4, such as snapper, haddock, or flounder (6 ounces/170 g each)
Unbleached all-purpose flour	½ cup (70 g)
Large eggs	2 large
Plain dried bread crumbs	1 cup (90 g)
Canola oil	½ cup (120 ml)
Salted butter	4 tablespoons (55 g)
Lemon	1
Flaky sea salt and pepper	

1. Cut the broccoli florets from the stem and cut the florets into bite-sized
   pieces. Peel the stem and cut it crosswise into ½-inch (12-mm) slices. Set aside.

   Don't waste broccoli stems. Peeled and cooked, they are as flavorful and tender as florets.

2. Pat the fish fillets dry with paper towels. Spread the flour in a wide, shallow
   bowl. Beat the eggs until blended in a second shallow bowl. Spread the bread
   crumbs in a third shallow bowl. One at a time, turn each fish fillet in flour,
   taking care to coat it evenly. Dip in the eggs to coat, and then in the bread

recipe continues ▸

crumbs, gently patting on the crumbs to help them adhere. Put the breaded fillets on a plate.

Don't let the fillets stand longer than 10 minutes, or the crumbs could start to get soggy.

3. Bring 3½ cups (840 ml) water to a boil in a medium saucepan for the broccoli as you get ready to fry the fish. When it boils, reduce the heat to a simmer.

4. Line a platter with paper towels and put it near the stove. Heat the oil and 2 tablespoons of the butter together in a large skillet over medium heat until the butter is melted and the foam starts to subside. In batches, add the fish fillets and cook, turning once, until they are golden brown all over and opaque in the center when pierced with the tip of a knife, about 6 minutes. Adjust the heat as needed so the fish is surrounded by bubbles in the oil but isn't browning too quickly.

Don't crowd the fillets in the skillet. If they don't fit all at once, cook them in two batches, adding more oil and butter to the skillet if needed. If you wish, keep the first batch warm in a preheated 200°F (100°C) oven while cooking the second batch.

5. Use a slotted spatula to transfer the fish to the paper towels to drain while you cook the broccoli.

6. Bring the simmering water back to a boil and season with a teaspoon or so of salt. Add the remaining 2 tablespoons butter and let it melt. Add the broccoli stems (they need to cook longer than the florets) and boil for 1 minute. Add the florets and cook until the broccoli is deep green and barely tender, 3 minutes more. Drain well.

7. Cut the lemon into wedges and place in a small bowl. Season the fish and broccoli with salt and pepper. Serve hot, passing the lemon separately.

TONKATSU CHICKEN WITH CARAMELIZED CARROTS

SERVES 4

One of the things that makes eating in Japan so fascinating is how dedicated cooks are to their craft, refining and perfecting a single dish for years or even decades. René and I visited a restaurant that specialized in tonkatsu, a breaded and fried cutlet, usually pork, served in a soft egg omelet atop a bowl of rice. It was amazing to see how carefully the chef worked, and we stayed at the counter for hours watching him, drinking beer and eating his perfectly fried food. This is a lacier, lighter dish than the breaded fish on page 183, with a little more kick, but the method is similar. I season the egg batter rather than the crumbs because the flavorings are less likely to burn this way, and they infuse the meat with flavor. Use a smooth rather than chunky chili paste.

CARAMELIZED CARROTS

Carrots	1 pound (455 g)
Salted butter	6 tablespoons (90 g)
Flaky sea salt	

BREADED CHICKEN

Unbleached all-purpose flour	½ cup (70 g)
Large eggs	2
Asian chili paste	2 tablespoons
Panko bread crumbs	1 cup (65 g)
Boneless, skinless chicken breast halves	4 (7 ounces/200 g) each
Canola oil	⅓ cup (75 ml)
Salted butter	2 tablespoons
Lemons	2

1. **Make the carrots:** Scrub the carrots under cold running water. Using a mandoline, V-slicer, or large knife, cut the carrots into very thin rounds. Melt 2 tablespoons of the butter in a medium saucepan over medium-low heat. Add the carrots and 3 tablespoons water. Slice the remaining 4 tablespoons

recipe continues ▸

(55 g) butter, scatter over the carrots, and cover tightly. Simmer until the butter has melted, the water has cooked away, and the carrots on the bottom are golden brown, about 10 minutes. Stir to move the top layer of carrots to the bottom of the pan, re-cover the pan, and cook until these carrots brown, about 5 minutes. Stir again and cook until most of the carrots are caramelized and very tender, about 5 minutes more.

If you think the carrots are scorching and not browning, add a tablespoon or so of water.

2. Preheat the oven to 200°F (100°C).

3. **While the carrots are cooking, cook the chicken:** Spread the flour in a wide, shallow bowl. Beat the eggs and chili paste well in a second shallow bowl. Spread the panko crumbs in a third shallow bowl. Pat the chicken dry with paper towels. One at a time, dip the breasts in the flour, making sure that each is coated all over, then in the eggs, letting the excess drip back into the bowl, then the panko crumbs. Put the breaded breast on a plate. Repeat with the remaining chicken.

4. Place a wire rack on a baking sheet or line the pan with a double layer of paper towels. Heat the oil and butter together in a large skillet over medium heat until the foam subsides. Without crowding the pan, add the chicken to the hot oil and cook until golden brown on the bottom, 3 to 4 minutes. You may need to cook the chicken in two batches. Flip the chicken and continue cooking for 3 to 4 minutes more, or until browned and cooked through. If you pierce the thickest part with the tip of a knife, there should be no sign of pink. Use a slotted spatula to transfer the chicken to the wire rack and keep warm in the oven while frying the remaining chicken.

Adjust the heat in the pan as needed so the oil around the chicken bubbles steadily but the batter doesn't burn.

5. Transfer the carrots to a serving bowl and season to taste with salt. Cut the lemons in half crosswise. Serve the chicken with the lemons and carrots.

DANNY'S FRIED CHICKEN WITH SPICED RICE

SERVES 4

When I was a kid, my mother always allowed me to choose my own birthday dinner, and every year I asked for fried chicken, a dish she learned to make from my American godfather, Danny. Double-coating and double-cooking ensures a sturdy, crisp crust and fully cooked meat without deep-frying. I pair it with savory flavored rice inspired by the infused rice pilafs of Morocco. You want the chicken piping-hot, so make the rice first; if you leave it covered in its pot, it will stay nice and hot.

SPICED RICE

Canola oil	2 teaspoons
Madras-style curry powder	1 tablespoon
Basmati rice	1 cup (200 g)
Dark seedless raisins	½ cup (75 g)
Fine sea salt	½ teaspoon

FRIED CHICKEN

Unbleached all-purpose flour	1½ cups (210 g)
Large eggs	3
Garlic cloves	5
Fine sea salt	½ teaspoon
Freshly ground black pepper	¼ teaspoon
Chicken pieces	3 to 4 pounds (1.4 to 1.8 kg) breasts, drumsticks, and thighs (8 pieces total)
Canola oil, for frying	3 cups (720 ml), or as needed

TO SERVE

Lemon	1
Banana	1 large

1. **Make the spiced rice:** Heat the oil in a medium saucepan over medium heat. Stir in the curry powder and cook until fragrant, about 30 seconds. Add the

recipe continues ▸

rice and stir well to coat with the flavored oil. Stir in 2 cups (480 ml) water along with the raisins and salt and bring to a boil over high heat. Reduce the heat to very low. Cover and simmer, until the surface is covered with small air pockets, about 15 minutes. Remove from the heat and let stand, covered.

Don't stir the rice once it is simmering, as that will make it sticky and lumpy.

2. As soon as the rice is simmering, spread ½ cup (70 g) of the flour in a wide, shallow bowl. Beat the eggs in a second shallow bowl. Crush the garlic cloves under the flat side of a knife and peel the garlic. Chop it finely. Mix the remaining 1 cup (140 g) flour, garlic, salt, and pepper in a deep bowl.

3. Pat the chicken dry with paper towels. One piece at a time, roll the chicken in the plain flour then coat in the eggs. Dredge the chicken in the seasoned flour and transfer it to a platter.

Use one hand for the first coating of flour and the eggs, then your other hand for the second dredging. Otherwise, you will end up with batter-coated hands in no time.

4. Preheat the oven to 350°F (180°C). Pour enough oil into a large, deep skillet to come about ½ inch (12 mm) up the sides of the pan and heat over medium heat until the oil is shimmering but not smoking. To check the oil temperature, stick the end of a wooden spoon into the oil—when the oil bubbles around the spoon, the oil is ready.

5. Carefully put the chicken pieces in the pan, cooking them in batches if needed. Cook, turning occasionally, until they are light brown all over, about 6 minutes. The thighs and drumsticks will probably be done before the breasts. Transfer the pieces to a large, rimmed baking sheet.

Adjust the heat as needed so the oil is bubbling but the chicken isn't getting too dark too quickly. You are only getting a nice crust on the chicken, not cooking it all the way through.

6. Bake the chicken until the crust is deep golden brown and a thigh shows no sign of pink when pierced in the thickest part with the tip of a small knife, about 20 minutes.

7. Drain the chicken on a paper towel–lined baking sheet. Scoop the rice into a serving bowl. Halve the lemon and squeeze the juice over the rice. Top with sliced banana. Serve the hot chicken with the rice.

ROASTED BABY BACK RIBS AND SWEET POTATOES

SERVES 6

Danish people are so obsessed with American-style barbecue that it's now easier to find ribs pre-smothered in sauce at our markets than plain ones. Everyone seems to have a theory about the best way to cook them but I think they taste best simply roasted in the oven with no sauce at all. When you do something this simple to good-quality meat, you really notice the different tastes and textures as you work the chewy meat off the bones: the way the crunchy caramelized outer bits contrast with the juicy, tender bites between the ribs. Baby back ribs cook much more quickly than larger spareribs, and they require absolutely no work—just throw them and the potatoes in the oven when you get home, and that's it. I always roast an extra rack for leftovers. If René walks in the house after work and can smell that we've made ribs and didn't leave a few for him, he is very disappointed. Any that he doesn't polish off go in the girls' lunch boxes, but no matter how many I make there are never many left over.

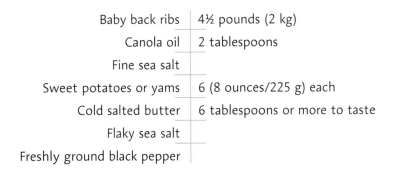

Baby back ribs	4½ pounds (2 kg)
Canola oil	2 tablespoons
Fine sea salt	
Sweet potatoes or yams	6 (8 ounces/225 g) each
Cold salted butter	6 tablespoons or more to taste
Flaky sea salt	
Freshly ground black pepper	

1. Preheat the oven to 400°F (200°C) with the oven racks in the center and top third of the oven.

2. Place the ribs, meaty side up, on a rimmed baking sheet. Try not to overlap the rib racks too much, as that will prevent the covered portions from browning. Rub with the oil and season generously with the fine sea salt.

   Don't worry if the rib racks overlap a little bit; they will shrink as they cook.

recipe continues ▸

3. Scrub the sweet potatoes under cold running water. Pierce each one a few times with a fork and place them on a second baking sheet.

4. Place the sweet potatoes on the upper oven rack and the ribs on the center rack. Bake until the ribs are a rich, reddish golden brown and tender when pierced with the tip of a knife, 1¼ hours to 1½ hours. The sweet potatoes should be very soft by this time. Remove from the oven and let rest for 5 minutes.

5. To serve, slice between the bones to separate the ribs and pile them onto a platter. Halve the sweet potatoes lengthwise and make a few lengthwise slits into the exposed flesh. Top the sweet potatoes with plenty of butter, flaky salt, and pepper and serve with the ribs.

ROAST CHICKEN AND POTATOES
WITH GARLIC AND THYME

SERVES 4 TO 6

There are as many recipes for roast chicken as there are cooks, and after trying what seems like all of them, this is the version I always come back to. The combination of garlic, lemon, and thyme is classic, and when you tip the pan, releasing the juices that have accumulated in the bird as it roasted, the aroma is just incredible. I roast a chicken at least once a week; it's probably my favorite thing to eat, though the broth I make from the carcass (page 149) is a close second, and another example of using something that might go to waste to make something really delicious. Try to find a large, free-range, organically raised chicken. To me, they have a better, firmer texture, and knowing the animal lived a better life and wasn't pumped full of drugs (or water) just makes it taste better. The oven temperature of 350°F (180°C) allows the chicken and potatoes to cook evenly without burning; at the end, the chicken is roasted for a few minutes at 425°F (220°C) to give it a beautiful brown skin.

Roasting chicken	1, about 5½ pounds (2.5 kg)
Lemon	1
Garlic cloves	12
Extra-virgin olive oil	4 tablespoons (60 ml)
Fine sea salt	1 teaspoon
Fresh thyme sprigs	About 14
Yukon Gold potatoes	10 medium

1. Take the chicken out of the fridge 1 to 2 hours before you plan to cook it. Wipe the chicken completely dry with paper towels.

   You want the chicken to be as close to room temperature as possible before it goes in the oven to ensure that it cooks evenly.

2. Preheat the oven to 350°F (180°C).

3. Cut the lemon into 6 wedges. Crush the garlic cloves with the flat side of your knife and discard the papery skins. Rub the chicken all over with 2 tablespoons

recipe continues ▸

of the oil and season inside and out with ½ teaspoon of the salt. Place the chicken in a roasting pan and stuff the body cavity with the lemon, garlic, and thyme.

Make sure you use a large roasting pan with plenty of room for the chicken and the potatoes. You want the potatoes to be able to make contact with the hot pan to get nice and crisp.

4. Scrub the potatoes and cut them in half lengthwise. Arrange the potatoes around the chicken, cut side down. Drizzle the potatoes with the remaining 2 tablespoons oil and sprinkle with the remaining ½ teaspoon salt.

5. Roast the chicken for about 1¼ hours. Raise the oven temperature to 425°F (220°C). Continue roasting until an instant-read thermometer inserted in the thickest part of the breast near the wing joint, but not touching a bone, reaches 175°F (80°C), about 30 minutes more.

Raising the heat near the end of cooking will give the bird the crisp brown skin you want.

6. Bring the chicken to the table right in the pan to serve. Twist off the wings and legs, then use a sharp knife to cut through the skin on the thighs; you should be able to pull them away from the carcass easily. Twist or cut the thighs off. Slice down either side of the breastbone to free the breast meat. Place the chicken and some of the potatoes onto each plate.

7. Now tilt the carcass so the lemony juices from the cavity run easily into the pan, and stir them together. Spoon some of the pan juices and the remaining potatoes onto each plate.

There will still be plenty of delicious chicken essence in the pan, so don't scrub it out. Instead make the gingery chicken broth on page 149.

PORCHETTA PORK BELLY WITH TRUFFLES

SERVES 6

Roasted pork belly, the same part of the animal used to make bacon (but not cured or smoked, as bacon is), is a traditional holiday or Sunday meal in Denmark. My grandmother made it every Christmas, and though she cooked the meat to death, she made the best cracklings. The scored fatty skin cooked up crisp and almost bark-like. I thought it was amazing and couldn't get enough of it. When I discovered porchetta, the Italian dish of rolled and roasted pork shoulder stuffed with herbs and garlic, I thought I could redeem this holiday staple by filling it with flavor. I took a high-low approach, combining a humble, fatty cut with upscale (but affordable) preserved truffles. The meat is cooked just until tender—it won't be meltingly soft like a braise, but it will have that irresistible crunchy fat layer keeping everything juicy. It's essential to let the roast rest before you slice it, or it will release all its juices and the meat will be dry. A green salad and roasted potatoes are so good with this.

Preserved black truffles	1 (2.8-ounce/80-g) jar
Boneless pork belly, with skin	1 (3 pounds/1.4 kg)
Fresh sage leaves	18 small leaves
Fine sea salt	
Potatoes	1½ pounds (680 g), thin-skinned, such as Yukon Gold
Canola oil	2 tablespoons
Freshly ground black pepper	
Special equipment	Kitchen twine, instant-read thermometer

1. Preheat the oven to 350°F (180°C).

2. Add the truffles and any liquid they were packed in to a blender or food processor and purée.

   Don't try to purée the truffles to a smooth paste; they should just be spreadable.

recipe continues ▸

3. Place the pork on your work surface, fat side up. Use a very sharp knife to score the skin in a crosshatch pattern, making the cuts about 1 inch (2.5 cm) apart. Be sure not to cut into the flesh, just through the skin and fat.

   Your knife must be very sharp to cut through the skin.

4. Turn the meat skin side down. Spread the whole surface with the truffle purée and arrange the sage leaves on top. Starting at a short edge, roll the pork belly into a fat log. Use kitchen twine to tie the log closed in 4 or 5 places. Season all over with salt.

5. Put the pork in a large roasting pan, seam side down. Peel the potatoes, cut them in half lengthwise, and scatter them around the pork. Drizzle the pork and potatoes with the oil. Turn the potatoes to coat them with oil, and arrange them cut side down. Season the potatoes with salt and pepper.

6. Roast until an instant-read thermometer inserted into the center of the pork reads 140° to 145°F (60° to 63°C), about 1½ hours.

   If the fat on the outside doesn't properly crisp, raise the oven temperature to 450°F (230°C) and you will see it change color and texture within about 5 minutes.

7. Transfer the meat to a large carving board and let it rest for 15 minutes. Keep the potatoes warm in the pan in the turned-off oven with the door ajar.

8. Cut off the twine and slice the roast crosswise. Arrange the meat on a platter, pouring any juices from the cutting board over the meat. Serve the porchetta with the potatoes.

   If you have a carving board with a channel to catch the meat juices, it's neater and you save all those good juices.

BEEF-GLAZED CELERY ROOT WITH BUTTERMILK SAUCE

MAKES 4 SERVINGS

One of the guiding principles of Noma is treating humble ingredients with the same respect we pay to more precious ingredients, and I had that in mind when I created this dish. Celery root cooked this way has as much presence on the plate as a slice of roast meat, it's so beefy and succulent. If you can find full-fat buttermilk, you'll get a thicker, more delicious sauce that doesn't separate, but if you can only get non-fat, it will still be good.

Celery root (celeriac)	2 (1 pound, 3 ounces/540 g) each
Canola oil, for the dish	1 tablespoon
Beef or veal demiglace	1 cup (240 ml)
Pine nuts	3 tablespoons
Salted butter	¾ cup plus 2 tablespoons (200 g)
Canola oil, for deep-frying	½ cup (120 ml)
Curly kale	2 large leaves
Parmigiano-Reggiano cheese	2 tablespoons freshly grated
Buttermilk	¼ cup (60 ml), preferably full-fat
Flaky sea salt	
Freshly ground black pepper	

1. Preheat the oven to 350°F (180°C),

2. Peel the celery roots, trimming off any gnarly roots. Rinse off any dirt and dry the roots with tea towels. Cut each root vertically into 4 slabs, each about ¾ inch (8 mm) wide, saving the end pieces for another use.

   Celery root has tough skin and a lot of small roots at one end, so use a sturdy vegetable peeler and a small sharp knife to remove the stubborn parts.

recipe continues ▸

3. With the oil, grease a baking dish just large enough to hold the slices in a single layer. Turn the slices to coat with the oil. Bake, uncovered, for 30 minutes. Flip the pieces and bake for another 30 minutes.

4. When the celery root has roasted for 1 hour, pour the demi-glace over the slices and raise the oven temperature to 400°F (200°C). Continue baking, basting occasionally, until the celery root is glazed and tender when pierced with the tip of a sharp knife and the demi-glace is reduced to a few tablespoons, 20 to 30 minutes. If the pan is starting to look dry, stir in 1 or 2 tablespoons hot water to keep the demi-glace from burning.

5. **While the celery root roasts,** heat a small, dry skillet over medium heat. Add the pine nuts and cook, shaking the pan every 20 to 30 seconds, until they are lightly toasted. Pour them into a small bowl to cool.

   Don't leave the pine nuts in the skillet—they will keep cooking and burn.

6. To start the brown butter sauce, cut the butter into tablespoons. Melt the butter in a medium saucepan over medium heat until the butter is melted and foamy. Continue to cook, stirring constantly with a whisk, until the butter smells nutty and the sediment on the bottom of the pan is light brown, about 2 minutes. Immediately pour the brown butter into a medium heatproof bowl and keep warm at the back of the stove.

   If the brown butter solidifies, just heat it gently until it melts again.

7. **Now, fry the kale:** Place a rimmed baking sheet lined with paper towels near the stove. Heat the oil in a small saucepan until it is shimmering. Tear the kale into pieces about the size of a quarter, discarding the tough stems. Add the kale to the oil a few pieces at a time—it will splatter, so be careful! Cook for just a second or two, until the kale is crisp. Using a slotted spoon, immediately lift the kale out of the oil and drain on paper towels. Repeat until all the kale bits are crisped.

8. Just before serving, sprinkle the celery root with the Parmigiano and bake until the cheese melts, about 5 minutes. Remove from the oven.

9. Gradually whisk the buttermilk into the warm brown butter. Divide the sauce among 4 shallow bowls. Add 2 celery root slices to each, along with a drizzle of the syrupy demi-glace from the pan. Sprinkle with the kale and pine nuts. Season to taste with salt and pepper and serve hot.

PAN-ROASTED CAULIFLOWER
WITH SESAME CRÈME FRAÎCHE

SERVES 4

Although none of us are full-time vegetarians, as a family we eat meatless meals once or twice a week. On those nights, sometimes it's nice to treat a vegetable the way you would treat a big cut of meat, roasting it whole. Getting the bottom of a cauliflower head golden brown gives it a meaty flavor. When it's the focus of the meal, go ahead and splurge on really excellent produce. After all, even the biggest, most expensive biodynamic organic head of cauliflower you can find is going to cost a lot less than an equivalent amount of beef. Serve this with a hearty grain salad with lots of herbs.

Cauliflower	1 medium (2 pounds/900 g)
Canola oil	3 tablespoons
Fresh thyme sprigs	5
Rosemary sprig	1
Garlic cloves	5
Salted butter	3 tablespoons (45 g)
Fine sea salt	
Freshly ground black pepper	
Crème fraîche	1 cup (225 ml)
Sesame oil	2 tablespoons
Lemon	1, for zesting

1. Trim the leaves from the cauliflower and use the tip of your knife to cut out the stem if it's still attached. Heat the oil in a medium Dutch oven just big enough to hold the cauliflower and heat until the oil is shimmering but not smoking. Add the cauliflower, stem end down. Scatter the thyme, rosemary, and unpeeled garlic cloves over and around the cauliflower.

   The thyme will sizzle and splatter, but this is normal.

recipe continues ▸

2. Cook the cauliflower over medium-high heat until the bottom is nicely browned, about 5 minutes. Turn the cauliflower over. Add ¼ cup of water and 2 tablespoons of the butter to the pot and swirl the pot to combine them. Top the cauliflower with the remaining 1 tablespoon butter. Cover tightly, reduce the heat to medium, and cook until the cauliflower is barely tender when pierced with the tip of a small knife, about 6 minutes. Remove from the heat and season with salt and pepper. Let the cauliflower stand, covered, for 5 minutes.

3. While the cauliflower is resting, put the crème fraîche in a small bowl. Gradually stir (do not whisk) in the sesame oil.

   Do not overmix the crème fraîche or it will loosen up. You want it nice and thick.

4. To serve, use a large knife to cut the cauliflower into quarters and transfer each quarter to a dinner plate. Spoon some of the crème fraîche next to each portion. Grate a bit of lemon zest over all and serve.

MUSSELS WITH CHORIZO

SERVES 6

Mussels are quite assertively flavored and can go head to head with other bold ingredients like chorizo and garlic. The creamy broth is the star here, so make sure to serve this with spoons as well as plenty of bread to sop up every drop. When I have a bottle of white Pineau des Charentes, a French fortified wine served as an aperitif, I substitute it for the vermouth, which really puts this over the top. I always eat the mussels with my hands, sipping a little sauce from the shell before scraping out the meat with my teeth. If that's a little too messy for you, use one of the empty shells like a tweezers, pinching it between your thumb and forefinger to pluck the meat from the shells.

Mussels	4 pounds (1.8 kg)
Canola oil	2 tablespoons
Onion	I large
Smoked Spanish chorizo	7 ounces (200 g)
Pancetta	7 ounces (200 g)
Garlic cloves	6
Plum (Roma) tomatoes	6 large
Fresh thyme sprigs	4
Bay leaves	2
Dry white vermouth	1 cup (240 ml)
Dry white wine	1 cup (235 ml)
Crème fraîche	1 cup (227 g)
Fresh flat-leaf parsley	5 or 6 sprigs
Crusty bread	For serving

1. Rinse the mussels under cold running water and drain them. If any are open, lightly tap them against the sink. If they close up, they can be cooked. If not, throw them away.

   Never try to force a closed mussel—raw or cooked—open.

recipe continues ▸

2. Heat the oil in a large pot over medium heat. Chop the onion and add it to the pot. Cook without stirring until it begins to brown on the bottom, about 3 minutes. While the onion is cooking, cut the chorizo and pancetta into ½-inch (12-mm) dice. Crush the garlic cloves with the flat side of your knife, discard the papery skins, and chop the garlic.

3. Add the garlic to the pot and stir just until fragrant. Move the onion and garlic to one side of the pot and add the chorizo and pancetta to the other side. Cook, stirring the chorizo and pancetta occasionally, until they are lightly browned and the fat has rendered, about 8 minutes.

4. To core the tomatoes easily, slice each downward next to but not through the stem. Make two angled cuts into the larger half to release the core and discard. Coarsely chop the tomatoes and add to the pot with the thyme and bay leaves. Cook until the tomatoes soften, about 2 minutes. Stir in the vermouth and wine and bring to a boil. Simmer, stirring often, until the liquid has reduced by about one-fourth and the tomatoes have broken down, about 10 minutes.

5. Raise the heat to high. Stir in the crème fraîche and bring to a simmer. Add the mussels, give them a good stir, and cover the pot. Cook for 5 to 6 minutes, giving the pot a vigorous shake now and then. After 5 minutes, check to see if the mussels have opened. If not, cover and cook another minute or so until almost all are open. Remove from the heat.

   Mussels are brilliant because they let you know they are done when they pop open.

6. Coarsely chop the parsley (you can include a bit of the tender stems if you want) and stir it in. Using tongs and a ladle, divide the mussels and broth among 6 shallow bowls. Serve with the bread to sop up the fantastic broth.

BRAISED PORK CHEEK RAGU

SERVES 6

Pork cheeks really benefit from long, slow braise and make a super-savory sauce for a cold-weather pasta meal. If you have a juicer, this is the perfect time to break it out and salvage any vegetables that are starting to look a bit sad; otherwise, you can get what you need for the braising liquid at any juice bar or in the refrigerated section of many large supermarkets. Pork shoulder could substitute for the cheeks, but if you can find them, they are fantastic cooked this way. I serve this over pasta but it would be equally good on polenta or mashed potatoes.

BRAISED PORK CHEEKS

Grapeseed or canola oil	2 tablespoons
Pork cheeks	2 pounds (910 g)
Shallots, large	2
Garlic cloves	8
Fresh thyme sprigs	6
Pilsner beer or pale ale	1 (12-ounce/366-ml) bottle
Tomatoes	1 pound (455 g)
Celery juice	½ cup (120 ml)
Apple juice, preferably from green tart apples	½ cup (120 ml)
Carrot juice	½ cup (120 ml)
Fine sea salt	
Freshly ground black pepper	
Pasta, long or short cuts	I pound (455 g)
Parmigiano-Reggiano cheese	1 cup (110 g), freshly grated

1. **Cook the pork cheeks:** Heat the oil in a large Dutch oven over medium-high heat. In batches, add the pork cheeks and cook, turning occasionally, until browned, about 5 minutes. Return all the meat to the pot.

recipe continues ▸

2. Peel the shallots. Crush the garlic cloves with the flat side of your knife and discard the papery skins. Cut the shallots and the garlic cloves in half lengthwise and put them on top of the pork along with the thyme. Add the beer and bring to a boil, scraping up the browned bits in the bottom of the Dutch oven with a wooden spoon. To core the tomatoes easily, slice downward next to but not through the stem. Make two angled cuts into the larger half to release the core and discard. Coarsely chop the tomatoes. Add them, along with the celery and apple and carrot juices, to the Dutch oven. Add some water, if necessary, to barely cover the pork and bring to a boil.

3. Preheat the oven to 275°F (135°C). Cover the pot with the lid and put it in the oven to cook for 2½ to 3 hours, or until very tender. Check on the meat every now and then to give it a little stir and be sure the liquid is still covering it (add water, if needed).

   Use a pair of tongs to give one of the cheeks a gentle squeeze; if the meat falls apart easily, it is done.

4. **Cook the pasta:** Bring a large pot of water to a boil over high heat. Add a tablespoon or so of salt. Stir in the pasta and cook, stirring every 2 minutes, according to the package directions until the pasta is al dente, about 8 minutes. Drain well.

5. While the pasta is cooking, use a fork or your tongs to break up the cheeks to make a lovely thick sauce. Discard any thyme stems you find.

6. Divide the pasta among bowls and top with the sauce. Pass the Parmigiano on the side.

MY MOTHER'S CHICKEN CURRY

MAKES 8 SERVINGS

I've always liked spicy food, and even when I didn't like it I wanted to. My brother was always daring me to try fiery dishes, and I would eat them, pretending to enjoy it while my mouth was on fire. Eventually, though, I came to crave the burn, which is probably why I am so fond of curries and chile blends. This is a relatively simple, light curry that doesn't involve as much chopping or long simmering as the lamb curry on page 217. Once you've made the curry blend, it's really just a simple stew that cooks without supervision, filling the house with amazing smells. Cooking the chicken pieces whole gives the curry lots of flavor, but I shred the meat and discard the skin and bones before serving to make it easier to eat. I finish this with a blend of chamomile and salt. It's not traditional, but the dried flowers have an earthiness similar to coriander seeds.

RED CURRY PASTE

Fresh red chiles	3, such as cayenne or Fresno
Shallot	1 small
Fresh ginger	1 (1½-inch/4-cm) piece
Garlic	5 cloves
Cumin seeds	2 teaspoons
Fennel seeds	2 teaspoons
Dried chamomile flowers	2 tablespoons (from loose tea or teabags)
Sweet paprika	2 teaspoons
Grapeseed or canola oil	6 tablespoons (90 ml), as needed
Chicken	3 to 4 pounds (1.4 to 1.8 kg) legs, thighs, breasts, and wings
Salted butter	2 tablespoons
Onions	4 medium
Ripe plum (Roma) tomatoes	2 pounds (910 g)
Tart green apples	4
Golden raisins	1½ cups (200 g)
Fine sea salt	
Freshly ground black pepper	

recipe continues ▸

RAITA

Cucumber	1
Fine sea salt	½ teaspoon
Plain Greek yogurt	2 cups (455 g)
Fresh mint	20 sprigs
Basmati rice	3 cups (600 g)
Fresh cilantro sprigs	40

1. **Make the curry paste:** Halve the chiles and remove the ribs and seeds. Chop the chiles finely. Peel and coarsely chop the shallot and ginger. Crush the garlic cloves under the flat blade of a knife, then peel and coarsely chop the garlic. Crush the cumin and fennel seeds with a mortar and pestle. Add the chopped chiles, shallot, ginger, garlic, and the crushed cumin and fennel to a blender or food processor. Add the chamomile and paprika and 3 tablespoons of the grapeseed oil. Process until smooth, adding more oil if needed to make a smooth paste.

   If you don't have a mortar and pestle, you can crush the spices on a chopping board under a heavy saucepan.

2. Heat a very large Dutch oven over medium-high heat. Add the remaining 3 tablespoons of oil and heat it.

3. In batches, add the chicken and cook, turning once, until golden brown on both sides, about 6 minutes. Transfer the pieces to a platter as they are browned.

4. Add the butter to the Dutch oven and let it melt. Chop the onions, adding them to the pot as you go, and cook without stirring until they are browned on the bottom, about 5 minutes. Stir well. Stir in the curry paste and let it cook, stirring occasionally, until it begins to stick to the bottom of the pot a bit, 1 to 2 minutes. Return the chicken and any juices on the platter to the pot. Add 3 cups (720 ml) water. Reduce the heat to low.

   Don't fill the pot with water! The tomatoes in the next step will release plenty of juice.

recipe continues ▶

INDIAN BREADS

India is famous for its breads, and most any of them would work well with this meal, including naan, paratha, and roti (or even pita bread), many of which you can find in well-stocked supermarkets. My favorite is freshly fried papadums. Cracker-like, crisp, and mildly spiced, these are made from lentil flour and are sold at Indian grocers. Deep-fry them as you would potato chips (page 29) until crisp, then drain on paper towels. Unlike most deep-fried foods, you can stack papadums while draining them without any risk of them losing their crunch.

5. To core the tomatoes easily, slice downward next to but not through the stem. Make two angled cuts into the larger half to release the core and discard. Squeeze the tomatoes a little to get out most of the seeds and chop the tomatoes into ½-inch (12-mm) pieces. Stir them into the pot. Peel, core, and cut the apples into 1-inch (2.5-cm) chunks. Stir the apples and raisins into the pot. Add a little more water, if needed, to barely cover the ingredients. Raise the heat to high and bring the curry to a boil. Season well with salt and pepper. Reduce the heat to low, cover the pot tightly, and simmer the curry for about 2 hours, until the chicken is almost falling off the bones.

    Stir the curry every now and then to keep the chicken and other ingredients from sticking.

6. **While the curry cooks, make the raita:** Peel the cucumber and cut it in half lengthwise. Use a spoon to scrape out the seeds. Cut the cucumber lengthwise into strips about ¼ inch (6 mm) thick. Now cut them crosswise into ¼-inch (6-mm) pieces. Toss with the ½ teaspoon salt in a colander. Let drain for 30 minutes. Rinse well and pat dry with a tea towel. Stir the cucumber, yogurt, and mint in a medium serving bowl. Cover and refrigerate until serving.

7. **About 30 minutes before you plan to serve, make the rice:** Combine the rice and 6 cups (1.4 L) water in a medium-large saucepan. Stir to combine, then bring to a boil over medium heat. Reduce the heat to low, cover the saucepan, and cook without disturbing until little air pockets appear on the top of the rice, about 15 minutes. Remove from the heat and let stand, covered, for 10 minutes.

    Don't stir the rice once it is simmering, or it will become sticky and gluey.

8. Just before you serve the curry, use tongs to pick out the pieces of chicken and, when cool enough to handle, pull the meat off the bones. Return the meat to the pot, discarding the skin and bones, and use the tongs to shred the meat into the sauce. Give the curry a little stir and taste it, adjusting the seasonings. Taste again and see what you think. You might want to add even more spices.

    If you feel you have gone overboard with spices, add a tablespoon of yogurt.

9. Chop the cilantro leaves and put them in a small bowl. Serve the curry on bowls of rice and pass the raita and cilantro on the side.

LAMB CURRY WITH RICE AND RAITA

SERVES 8 TO 10

Curry is such a catch-all name, and while both this and the chicken dish on page 213 are curries, they are very different from each other. This one uses lemongrass and cardamom to brighten long-cooked lamb. Swapping veggies for the usual apples and raisins makes this a more savory, less-sweet dish, too. The eggplant and zucchini cook down almost to a puree that is enriched with cashew cream.

This dish is a bit labor intensive, but it serves a lot of people, so bust it out when you have a large crowd. You can make the curry ahead of time and reheat it gently when you start to make the rice. Leftovers freeze well, so you can bank a few extra weeknight meals. For this, you want lamb shoulder, not meat from the leg, which would become tough and dry.

CURRY PASTE

Lemongrass	2 stalks
Fresh green chiles	3, such as jalapeño or serrano
Fresh ginger	1 (2-inch/5-cm) piece
Shallots	2 large
Garlic cloves	6
Coriander seeds	2 tablespoons
Cumin seeds	2 tablespoons
Cardamom seeds	2½ teaspoons
Ground turmeric	4 teaspoons
Sweet paprika	2 tablespoons
Salt	1 teaspoon
Water	¼ cup (50 ml)

CURRY

Canola oil	⅓ cup (80 ml), or as needed
Boneless lamb shoulder	4 pounds (1.8 kg), well trimmed and cut into 1½-inch (4-cm) pieces
Fine sea salt	
Pepper	
Lamb neck bones	1½ pounds (680 kg)

recipe continues ▸

Eggplant	1 medium
Zucchini	3 (about 1 pound/455g)
Onions	1 large
Raw cashews	8 ounces (225 g)
Fresh lemon juice	2 tablespoons or to taste

RAITA

Cucumber	2
Fine sea salt	½ teaspoon
Fresh mint	20 sprigs
Plain Greek yogurt	1 cup (225 g)

Basmati rice	3 cups (600 g)
Fresh cilantro leaves	40
Prepared mango chutney	1 cup

1. **Make the curry paste:** Peel off the tough outer layer of the lemongrass and coarsely chop the tender white inner bulb. Halve the chiles, scrape out and discard the seeds and ribs, and coarsely chop chiles. Peel and coarsely chop the ginger and shallot. Crush the garlic cloves under the flat side of a knife, discard the papery skins, and coarsely chop the garlic. Crush the coriander, cumin, and cardamom seeds with a mortar and pestle, or on a chopping board under a heavy saucepan. Put them all in a blender with the turmeric, paprika, and salt and add 2 tablespoons of water. Process until smooth, adding a little more water if needed to make a thick paste.

2. **Make the curry:** Heat 3 tablespoons of the oil in a very large Dutch oven over medium-high heat. In batches, add the pieces of lamb shoulder and cook, turning occasionally and adding more oil as needed, until browned, about 5 minutes. Season with salt and pepper. Transfer the lamb to a bowl and brown the lamb bones the same way. Add to the bowl. Add the curry paste to the pot and cook, stirring occasionally, until it begins to stick, 1 to 2 minutes.

3. Return the lamb, bones, and any juices to the Dutch oven and stir to coat with the curry mixture.

   Cooking the paste before you add liquid to the pot helps bring out the flavor of the spices.

4. Add just enough water to almost cover the lamb, about 3 cups (720 ml). Bring to a gentle simmer over medium heat. As it heats, cut the unpeeled eggplant and zucchini into 1-inch (2.5-cm) chunks. Add them to the Dutch oven, stir, then add more water if needed to just barely cover the ingredients.

   The vegetables will give off a fair amount of liquid, so don't add too much water.

5. Bring to a boil over high heat, then reduce the heat to low and cover tightly. Simmer, stirring occasionally, until the meat is very tender, about 1½ hours.

   While the curry is cooking, make the cashew purée, raita, and rice.

6. **Make the raita:** Peel the cucumbers and cut them in half lengthwise. Use a spoon to scrape out the seeds. Cut the cucumbers lengthwise into strips about ¼ inch (6 mm) thick, then crosswise into ¼-inch (6-mm) pieces. Toss with the ½ teaspoon salt in a colander. Let drain for 30 minutes. Rinse well and pat dry with a tea towel.

   Salting and draining the cucumber will draw out its liquid so your raita isn't watery.

7. Coarsely chop the mint and place in a medium serving bowl. Add the cucumber and yogurt, and stir gently to combine. Cover and refrigerate until serving.

8. **About 45 minutes before you plan to serve, make the rice:** Combine the rice and 6 cups (1.4 L) water in a medium-large saucepan. Stir to combine, and then bring to a boil over medium heat. Reduce the heat to low, cover the saucepan, and cook without disturbing until little air pockets appear on the top of the rice, about 25 minutes. Remove from the heat and let stand, covered, for 10 minutes.

   Don't stir the rice once it is simmering, or it will become sticky and lumpy.

9. **Make the cashew puree:** Heat the remaining 3 tablespoons oil in a large skillet over medium-high heat until it is shimmering but not smoking. Chop the onions and add to the skillet with the cashews. Cook until the onions are browned, 8 to 10 minutes, stirring often to prevent them from scorching or sticking. Remove from the heat and let the mixture cool a bit.

10. Fish the neck bones out of the Dutch oven. Pull off any meat and return it to the pot, discarding the bones. Carefully pour the cooking liquid into a bowl. In two batches, transfer the onion/cashew mixture to a blender and

recipe continues ▸

add 2 cups (475 ml) of the cooking liquid. With the lid slightly ajar to let the steam escape, puree until smooth and creamy. Stir the cashew puree into the curry and bring to a simmer. If it seems too thick, thin it out with a bit of the remaining cooking liquid. Season well with salt and pepper to taste.

11. Depending on the age and intensity of your spices, the curry can taste a little bland at this point. Taste the curry, then smell the spices, and add what you think it is missing, as well as more salt and pepper. Keep tasting and adding more spices until you're happy with the level of seasoning.

    If you think that you have maybe gone a little overboard with spices, don't worry; the raita will mellow the heat.

12. Chop the cilantro leaves (you can use some of the tender stems, too) and put them in a small serving bowl. Serve the curry with the raita, rice, and chutney, with the cilantro for sprinkling.

DESSERTS

Just as a roasting chicken coming from the oven can fill the house with a scent that gets everyone excited, the smell of butter and sugar warms you and makes you happy. That's why I love baking, and have come up with a repertoire of fast tarts, easy cakes, and assorted sweets that are weekday-friendly and decadent enough for any gathering. Most of the desserts in this section are quite simple, so using the very best ingredients makes all the difference. Organic whole milk, real butter, and heavy cream are all essential to my desserts, as are real vanilla beans, fresh eggs, and good-quality bittersweet chocolate. When you have tasted ice cream that is little more than fresh cream and milk, organic egg yolks, and the seeds of the best vanilla beans you can find, or taken a bite of the fudgy, dense brownies with undertones of caramel and bits of white chocolate, your ideas about what desserts should taste like will change forever. And trust me: you'll feel good about every bite.

Another recurring theme that weaves through many of these desserts is nuts, nut pastes, and nut flours. I use them to transform the basic batter for the Do-It-All cake into a rich layered cake, to give depth to chocolate chip cookies, and create an earthy filling for a fruit tart. It's amazing what a range of flavors and textures they contribute to all kinds of baked goods, reason enough to keep a few kinds in your baking pantry.

FRUIT DESSERTS

THREE-FRUIT CRUMBLE

SERVES 6 TO 8

This recipe is all about textures. Sprinkling the topping with butter and sugar helps it form an extra-crisp crust; when you crack through with your spoon the tender crumbs and soft fruit are revealed beneath it. The little clusters of topping bake down into the filling, absorbing the fruit juices to create a perfectly balanced mouthful, especially with a dollop of tangy crème fraîche. This is a perfect way to use overripe or bruised fruits, as fruit is actually at its most flavorful and sweetest when it is just on the edge of going bad! Just be sure to cut away and discard any part that is discolored or mushy. If your fruit is not all that sweet, add 2 more tablespoons of sugar to the filling. This is so good the next day.

CRUMBLE TOPPING

Unbleached all-purpose flour	1½ cups (210 g)
Sugar	¾ cup (150 g)
Fine sea salt	Pinch
Cold salted butter	5 tablespoons (75 g)

FILLING

Cold salted butter	1½ tablespoons
Rhubarb	3 stalks
Mango	1
Strawberries	10 large
Sugar	4 tablespoons (50 g)
Fine sea salt	Pinch
Crème fraîche	1 cup (240 g), for serving (optional)

1. Preheat the oven to 350°F (180°F).

2. **First, make the crumble topping:** Whisk the flour, sugar, and salt together in a medium bowl. Cut the butter into small cubes, add to the bowl, and toss

recipe continues ▶

to coat. Using your fingertips, rub the butter into the flour mixture until the ingredients are combined and you can gather the mixture into a ball.

Move quickly when working the butter with your fingers. The heat of your hands can warm up the butter too much and make the topping heavy and greasy, not light and crisp.

3. **Make the filling:** Cut the butter into small cubes and set aside. Cut the rhubarb into ⅓-inch (1-cm) slices and place in a 9-inch (23-cm square) baking dish. Slice down on either side of the flat mango pit and score the flesh attached to the skin in 1-inch (2.5-cm) squares. Use a spoon to scoop the mango cubes off the peel into the dish. (You can either cut the remaining mango off the pit or just do as I do and eat it yourself.) Remove the hulls from the strawberries, cut the berries in half, and add to the baking dish.

To hull the strawberries, use the point of a small, sharp knife to dig out the stem and leaves; slicing across the top of each berry wastes too much fruit!

4. Add half of the butter cubes and 3 tablespoons of the sugar to the pan and toss to mix with the fruit. Sprinkle with the salt. Crumble the topping mixture over the fruit, leaving some larger chunks. Scatter the remaining butter pieces over the crumble topping and sprinkle with the remaining 1 tablespoon sugar.

5. Place the dish on a baking sheet to catch any drips and bake until the fruit filling is bubbling and the topping is browned, 35 to 50 minutes.

Let cool for at least 30 minutes. Serve warm, at room temperature, or chilled with the crème fraîche.

CONGRATULATIONS: YOU CAN MAKE A FRUIT CRUMBLE

Don't be shy about mixing and matching your favorite fruits. I've learned that some of the most unexpected combinations turn out to be the best. This topping is easy to double, and it freezes very well. It's great to have on hand for unexpected guests or when you have a bunch of fruit that is about to go bad. Try these combinations or come up with your own.

• 4 ripe peaches, peeled, pitted, and cut into ½-inch (12-mm) wedges and 1 pint blueberries
• 1 pint blackberries and 3 barely ripe peeled pears
• 2 Golden Delicious apples (peeled, cored, and cut into chunks), 2 cups (330 g) bite-sized fresh pineapple chunks, and ½ pint (1 cup) fresh pitted cherries

DANISH APPLE DESSERT

SERVES 6

In Denmark this is called a cake, but it's really more like a trifle, with layers of whipped cream and crushed cookies on a base of caramelized apple puree. Whatever you call it, it's light and delicious and easy to make. You can also double the recipe and make it in a large bowl, trifle-style, but don't assemble it until just before serving, as the cookies will lose their crunch. This recipe makes about 20 large cookies and you won't need them all for the topping, so you'll have some left over for snacking and lunch boxes. If you haven't been saving your scraped vanilla bean pods this is the perfect way to use them up. Otherwise, just use a whole fresh one, slitting it and scraping the seeds over the apples.

APPLESAUCE

Apples	4 pounds (1.8 kg), such as Jonagold or Mutsu
Scraped vanilla beans	2

ALMOND COOKIES

Almond paste	1 (7- to 8-ounce/200- to 215-g) package
Sugar	2 cups (400 g)
Large egg whites	3
Unbleached all-purpose flour	1½ tablespoons
Baking powder	½ teaspoon
Heavy cream	1½ cups (360 ml)

1. **The filling needs to chill, so make it first:** Peel, quarter, and core the apples. Put the apples in a large, heavy pot. Place the vanilla beans on top. Cover the pot and cook over medium-high heat, without stirring, until the apples are lightly browned on the bottom, about 3 minutes.

   Caramelizing the apples brings out their sweetness without any added sugar. It's okay if some of them scorch a tiny bit.

2. Stir the apples, scraping the browned surfaces from the bottom of the pan. Reduce the heat to very low, cover the pan, and cook, stirring occasionally,

recipe continues ▸

until the apples have softened into a chunky purée, 45 to 60 minutes. If the apples start to stick or scorch, add a few tablespoons of water to the pot and stir to loosen them. Let the apples cool a bit, then cover and refrigerate until chilled, at least 2 hours or up to 1 day.

3. **Make the cookies:** Preheat the oven to 350°F (180°C) with the racks in the top third and center of the oven. Line two large, rimmed baking sheets with parchment paper.

4. Crumble the almond paste into a food processor. Add the sugar and process until well combined. Transfer to a medium bowl. Using an electric mixer on medium speed, beat in the egg whites one at a time, making sure each white is incorporated before adding another. Beat until smooth. With the mixer on low speed, mix in the flour and baking powder just until combined.

   If you don't have a food processor, grate the almond paste into a medium bowl using the large holes of a box grater and stir in the sugar.

5. Scrape the cookie batter into a pastry bag fitted with a plain ½-inch (12-mm) tip or a large zip-top plastic bag with the corner snipped off. Pipe out 2-inch (5-cm) mounds of the batter, leaving about 3 inches (7.5 cm) between them. The cookies will spread in the oven. Bake until golden brown and crackly, about 15 minutes. Let the cookies cool completely on the baking sheets. They will fall and crack, but that's okay, as they will be crumbled later.

   Don't try to remove the cookies from the parchment paper until they have cooled completely or they will stick and break.

6. Whip the cream in a large bowl with an electric mixer on high speed just until it thickens and begins to form soft peaks. It should be slightly fluid, not stiff and fluffy.

7. Divide the applesauce among 6 serving bowls and top with the whipped cream on the opposite side. Coarsely crumble 1 or 2 cookies over each serving. Serve immediately.

   Leftover cookies can be stored in an airtight container at room temperature for up to 5 days.

OLD-FASHIONED APPLE TART

SERVES 8

There is something grandma-style homey about apple desserts, and fortunately it's possible to get good apples year-round. We always keep a bowl of apples on the counter for the kids, so when I have to make a spur-of-the-moment dessert, this is the recipe I often turn to. If you find the idea of rolling out pastry dough intimidating, you'll find this crust, which is pressed into the pan with your fingers, very reassuring, and a layer of almond paste between the fruit and the crust helps keep the bottom from becoming soggy. It is so good warm topped with vanilla ice cream or crème fraîche, but it's almost as good cooled to room temperature. This is best made with an apple that is firm and not too sweet, such as Golden Delicious. Before buying, press an apple firmly with your fingertip; if you can make a dent (as if you were pressing on Styrofoam), choose another variety.

TART DOUGH

Cold salted butter	½ cup (110 g)
Unbleached all-purpose flour	1½ cups (210 g)
Fine sea salt	Pinch
Ice water	4 tablespoons (60 ml), as needed

Apples	3 to 4, such as Golden Delicious
Almond paste	1 (7- to 8-ounce/200- to 225-g) package
Flaky sea salt	For sprinkling
Cold salted butter	2 tablespoons
Sugar	2 tablespoons

1. **Make the tart dough:** Cut the butter into small cubes. Put the flour and salt in a medium bowl, add the flour, and toss to coat the butter. Using your fingertips, rub the butter into the flour—the mixture will look like coarse crumbs with some larger flakes.

   You can also pulse the flour and butter together in a food processor until the mixture looks like coarse crumbs with pea-sized bits of butter, then transfer the mixture to a bowl.

recipe continues ▸

2. Stirring with a fork, sprinkle in the water, 1 tablespoon at a time, just until the mixture clumps together and can be gathered into a ball. It should feel something like modeling clay, but not wet. If it's too dry, mix in more ice water by the half-teaspoon.

3. Break up the dough into walnut-sized chunks and scatter them into a 9-inch (23-cm) tart pan with a removable bottom. Using your fingers, press the dough evenly onto the bottom and up the sides of the pan, making sure it isn't too thick where the bottom meets the sides. It should protrude just a bit above the rim of the pan. Refrigerate the tart shell while the oven preheats.

   Keep pressing and spreading the bits of dough with your fingers to join them together and line the pan as evenly as possible.

4. Preheat the oven to 375°F (190°C).

5. Pierce the dough all over with a fork. Place the pan on a baking sheet. Line the bottom and sides of the dough with a large piece of parchment paper and fill it about halfway with dried beans to hold the paper in place.

   Weighting the crust will help keep the sides of your tart shell from slipping down as it bakes. You can reuse the beans for baking; just cool them before storing in a jar or plastic bag.

6. Bake until the visible edges of the dough look drier and set, about 15 minutes. Remove the pan from the oven. Lift off the paper and beans, and return the pan to the oven. Bake until the crust is barely browned, 7 to 10 minutes. Remove from the oven, but leave the oven on.

7. Peel and quarter the apples. Cut out the cores from each quarter, then thinly slice the apples about ⅛ inch (3 mm) thick.

8. Cut the almond paste into walnut-sized chunks. Press and pat the chunks into flat disks and use them to evenly line the bottom of the crust, breaking up the disks to fill in any empty spots as needed. Lightly sprinkle the almond paste with flaky salt. Arrange the apples in overlapping concentric circles on top. Fill in the center with apple slices arranged in a casual "flower" pattern. Cut the butter into small cubes, scatter them over the apples, and sprinkle with the sugar.

   Taste an apple slice before filling the tart shell. You may want to sprinkle a couple more (or fewer) teaspoons of sugar onto the slices, depending on how tart they are.

recipe continues ▸

9. Return to the oven and bake until the apples are tender and the tips are browned, 50 to 60 minutes. Let the tart cool on a wire rack for at least 20 minutes. Remove the sides of the pan and serve warm.

CONGRATULATIONS: YOU'VE MADE A TART SHELL

This is an endlessly versatile dough, which is why I use it to make everything from quiche to the richest desserts. You could also press the dough into individual tartlet pans. Here are a few more ideas for filling a partially baked tart shell:

FOR A FRUIT TART

After removing the beans, bake the tart shell until golden brown and fully baked, about 10 minutes more. Let cool, then fill the tart shell with your favorite berry preserves and then with a layer of fresh berries. Serve with whipped cream or crème fraîche.

FOR A CHOCOLATE TART

Fully bake the tart shell as for the fruit tart, above. For a chocolate ganache filling, heat ¾ cup (180 ml) heavy cream to a simmer and remove from the heat. Add 6 ounces (170 g) chopped bittersweet chocolate to the saucepan and let stand until softened, 2 to 3 minutes. Whisk until smooth and pour into the shell. Refrigerate until firm. Top with fruit (sliced bananas or pitted cherries are nice) and serve.

APRICOT TART
WITH FRANGIPANE

SERVES 8

Confession: Eating raw peaches and apricots has never been my thing. Somehow the furry skin just sets my teeth on edge. Cooked fruit, though, is an entirely different matter, and I think peaches, nectarines, plums, and especially apricots are amazing in a nutty frangipane filling. As it bakes, the frangipane puffs up around the sweet, tangy fruit, making a very elegant-looking tart. It's the kind of dessert that makes you think "Hmm, maybe I could open a bakery!" Serve it with vanilla ice cream or lightly sweetened whipped cream if you want.

TART DOUGH

Cold salted butter	½ cup (110 g)
Unbleached all-purpose flour	1½ cups (210 g)
Fine sea salt	⅛ teaspoon
Ice water	3 tablespoons, as needed

FRANGIPANE FILLING

Raw almonds	1 cup (110 g)
Sugar	½ cup plus 1 tablespoon (125 g)
Heavy cream	⅓ cup (75 ml)
Egg yolks	2 large
Fine sea salt	Pinch
Apricots	6 to 8

1. **Make the tart dough:** Cut the butter into small cubes. Put the butter and salt in a medium bowl, add the flour, and toss to coat the butter. Using your fingertips, rub the butter into the flour—the mixture will look like coarse crumbs with some larger flakes.

   You can also pulse the flour and butter together in a food processor until the mixture looks like coarse crumbs with pea-sized bits of butter, then transfer the mixture to a bowl.

recipe continues ▶

2. Stirring with a fork, sprinkle in the water just until the mixture clumps together and can be gathered into a ball. It should feel something like modeling clay, but not wet. If it's too dry, mix in more ice water by the half-teaspoon.

3. Lightly butter a 9-inch (23-cm) tart pan with a removable bottom. Break up the dough into walnut-sized chunks, and with your fingers press it evenly onto the bottom and up the sides of the pan, being sure it isn't too thick where the bottom meets the sides. It should protrude about ⅛ inch (3 mm) above the rim of the pan. Refrigerate the tart shell while the oven preheats.

   Keep pressing and spreading the bits of dough with your fingers to join them together and line the pan as evenly as possible.

4. Preheat the oven to 375°F (190°C).

5. Pierce the dough all over with a fork. Place the pan on a baking sheet. Line the bottom and sides of the dough with a large piece of parchment paper and fill it about halfway with dried beans to hold the paper in place.

   Weighting the crust will help keep the sides of your tart shell from slipping down as it bakes. You can reuse the beans for baking; just cool them before storing in a jar or plastic bag.

6. Bake until the visible edges of the dough look drier and set, about 15 minutes. Remove the pan on the baking sheet from the oven. Lift off the parchment paper with the beans and set them aside. Return the baking sheet and pan to the oven and bake until the crust is barely browned, 7 to 10 minutes. Remove from the oven.

7. **Make the filling:** Process the almonds and sugar in a food processor until the mixture is finely ground. With the machine running, add the cream, egg yolks, and salt and process until the frangipane is smooth.

8. Halve the apricots lengthwise and remove the pits. Spread the frangipane in the crust. Top with the apricots, pitted sides down.

9. Bake until the filling is lightly puffed and golden brown, 30 to 35 minutes. Let cool completely on a wire rack. Remove the sides of the pan, cut into wedges, and serve.

DO-IT-ALL CAKE

MAKES 1 LOAF CAKE; SERVES 8 TO 10

This may be the most valuable recipe in the whole book, because once you are comfortable making it, it is the gateway to a host of rather impressive desserts that use this simple batter as a foundation. It's so easy to dress up for any occasion by adding fruits and berries to the batter or adding a topping, or even just baking it in a different pan. Don't worry that your family or guests will think you're always making the same old thing; on the contrary, they'll be impressed by how many desserts you have in your repertoire! Only you will be in on the secret that they all start with this very basic loaf cake recipe. I don't mean to sell this cake short by calling it basic, by the way. It's based on a recipe given to me by the super-talented chef Rosio Sanchez, who worked in the kitchen at Noma and now has her own place in Copenhagen. Her version included lemon oil and other restaurant-y ingredients, so I stripped it down to these bare essentials. Since it uses so few ingredients, make sure they are the best quality you can find. Using a vanilla bean rather than extract, for example, does make a difference here.

Unbleached all-purpose flour	1¾ cups (245 g), plus more for dusting
Baking powder	1½ teaspoons
Fine sea salt	¼ teaspoon
Salted butter	½ cup (110 g), at room temperature
Sugar	1½ cups (300 g)
Vanilla bean	1
Large eggs	2 large, at room temperature
Heavy cream	¾ cup (175 ml)
Flaky sea salt	¼ teaspoon

1. Preheat the oven to 350°F (180°C). Lightly butter a 9 × 5-inch (23 × 12-cm) loaf pan. Line the bottom with parchment paper.

2. Whisk the 1¾ cups (245 g) flour, the baking powder, and the sea salt in a medium bowl. Put the butter and sugar in another medium bowl. Use the tip of a small knife to split the vanilla bean lengthwise then scrape the seeds into

recipe continues ▸

the bowl, saving the pod for another use. Beat the mixture with an electric mixer on high speed until it is pale, 4 to 5 minutes.

Don't shortchange this step. Because of the high proportion of sugar to butter, this will take some time to change color and texture.

3. Beat in the eggs, one at a time, beating well after each addition until light and fluffy. With the mixer on low speed, add the flour mixture in thirds, alternating with two additions of the cream, and beat, scraping down the sides of the bowl as needed, just until smooth.

4. Spread the batter evenly in the prepared pan and sprinkle the top with the flaky sea salt.

5. Bake until a wooden toothpick inserted in the center of the cake comes out clean and the top has a nice golden color, 50 minutes to 1 hour.

6. Let the cake cool in the pan on a wire rack for 10 minutes. Invert the cake onto the rack, remove the paper, and turn the cake right side up to cool completely.

BRANDIED PLUM CAKE

SERVES 8 TO 10

*If you needed more proof of the versatility of my basic cake batter, this dense,
moist dessert with fresh and dried plums and a crumble topping will make my case.
It's a cross between a cake and a pudding, and it tastes so good when it's not completely set
in the middle—almost like licking the cake batter bowl (but without the guilt and the raw
eggs!). It's the kind of thing I serve when I know we will be sitting around the table for some
time after the main course, talking, drinking wine, maybe having a little cheese. Once we've
digested a bit, I would bring this out. You could make this with all fresh plums or only
prunes, but I think the combination of chewy and soft fruit is what makes it interesting.*

Plums	2 large
Pitted prunes	1 cup (170 g)
Brandy or Armagnac	1 cup (240 ml), as needed

CRUMBLE

Unbleached all-purpose flour	1 cup (140 g)
Sugar	⅓ cup (65 g)
Fine sea salt	Pinch
Salted butter	5 tablespoons (70 g), at room temperature

CAKE LAYER

Unbleached all-purpose flour	1¾ cups (245 g)
Baking powder	1½ teaspoons
Fine sea salt	¼ teaspoon
Unsalted butter	½ cup (110 g), at room temperature
Granulated sugar	1½ cups (300 g)
Large eggs	2, at room temperature
Vanilla beans	1½
Heavy cream	¾ cup (175 g)
Cold salted butter	2 tablespoons
Sugar	2 tablespoons

recipe continues ▸

1. Pit the fresh plums and chop them into bite-sized pieces. Cut the prunes in half. Combine the plums and prunes in a small bowl and cover with the brandy. Cover and let stand at room temperature for at least 2 hours or up to 24 hours.

   Soaking the fresh plums in liqueur gives even out-of-season fruit a flavor boost.

2. **Make the crumble:** Whisk the flour, sugar, and salt in a medium bowl. Slice the butter and add it to the flour mixture. Using your fingertips, rub the mixture together until it is well combined and holds together when squeezed in your fist. Set aside at room temperature.

3. **Make the cake layer:** Preheat the oven to 350°F (180°C). Lightly butter a 9 × 13-inch (23 × 33-cm) baking pan.

4. Sift the flour, baking powder, and salt into a bowl. Beat the butter and sugar in a large bowl with an electric mixer on high speed until pale, about 4 minutes. Beat in the eggs, one at a time, until light and fluffy. Use the tip of a small knife to split the vanilla beans lengthwise, then scrape the seeds into the batter, saving the pods for another use. With the mixer on low speed, add the flour mixture in thirds, alternating with two additions of the cream, scraping down the bowl as needed, and mix until smooth. Spread the batter in the pan.

5. Strain the fruit through a sieve set over a bowl, reserving the soaking liquid. Scatter the soaked fruits over the cake batter and use a spoon to push them down into the batter. Spread the crumble topping over the batter, leaving a few large pieces. Cut the cold butter into small cubes. Dot the crumble with the butter and sprinkle with the sugar.

6. Bake until the cake is golden brown and a wooden toothpick inserted in the center of the cake (avoid the fruit!) comes out with moist crumbs, 40 to 45 minutes. Set the pan on a wire rack to cool. Serve it slightly warm or cooled to room temperature, with a drizzle of the soaking liquid.

   I love this cake when it is slightly undercooked with a very moist center. If you prefer, bake it for about 55 minutes, or until it is completely baked and the crumbs on the toothpick are dry. It is super-delicious either way.

DANISH DREAM CAKE

MAKES 12 SERVINGS

*Every Danish kid grows up eating dream cakes as an after-school treat, and you will find
them at just about any bakery. I thought it would be fun to make a version for adults.
The super-sweet, sticky coconut topping is the best part, and it keeps the cake very moist.
I've made it in a 9-inch square pan, but you could make individual dream cakes by baking
the batter and topping in muffin tins and reducing the cooking time by 5 minutes.*

CAKE LAYER

Unbleached all-purpose flour	1¾ cups (245 g)
Baking powder	1½ teaspoons
Fine sea salt	½ teaspoon
Salted butter	½ cup (110 g), at room temperature
Sugar	1½ cups (300 g)
Vanilla bean	1
Large eggs	2 large, at room temperature
Heavy cream	¾ cup (175 ml)

TOPPING

Salted butter	¾ cup plus 2 tablespoons (200 g)
Whole milk	Scant ½ cup (100 ml)
Light brown sugar	1½ cups (300 g) packed
Granulated sugar	1 cup (200 g)
Desiccated coconut flakes	2 cups (200 g)

1. **Make the cake layer:** Preheat the oven to 350°F (180°C). Lightly butter a
   9 × 9-inch (23 × 23-cm) baking pan.

2. Whisk the flour, baking powder, and the salt in a small bowl. Put the butter
   and sugar in a medium bowl. With the tip of a small knife, split the vanilla
   bean lengthwise, then scrape the seeds into the bowl, saving the pod for
   another use. Beat the mixture with an electric mixer on high speed until
   it is pale, 3 to 4 minutes.

recipe continues ▸

3. Beat in the eggs, one at a time, beating well after each addition until light and fluffy. With the mixer on low speed, add the flour mixture in thirds, alternating with two additions of the cream, and beat, scraping down the sides of the bowl as needed, just until smooth.

4. Spread the batter evenly in the pan. Bake just until the top is browned and the center feels almost, but not quite, set when pressed with a fingertip, about 30 minutes.

5. **While the cake bakes, make the topping:** Melt the butter in a medium saucepan over medium-high heat. Add the milk and heat until it is simmering. Stir in the brown sugar and granulated sugar and bring to a boil, stirring often. Stir in the coconut. Reduce the heat to medium-low and simmer, stirring almost constantly, until the sugar has dissolved, about 2 minutes.

   Be sure your coconut is not the sweetened flaked kind; the topping is sweet enough as is.

6. Remove the cake from the oven and immediately use a wooden skewer to poke holes all over the surface. Pour the topping evenly over the cake, using the back of a spoon to spread it into the corners. Return the cake to the oven and bake until the topping is set and has turned a shade or two darker, about 15 minutes.

7. Place the pan on a wire rack and let the cake cool completely. Cut into squares and serve.

DOUBLE-HAZELNUT PRALINE CAKE

SERVES 8

Playing with the flour component is yet another way to vary my basic Do-It-All Cake recipe and substituting nut meal for part of the wheat flour results in a cake with a distinctly earthy character. To really highlight the hazelnut notes, I frost the fully baked cake with a creamy hazelnut-praline. You'll find many recipes that recommend removing the skins from hazelnuts, and if you want to do that (or if you can buy skinless hazelnuts), be my guest. I've always considered that an unnecessary extra step (the kind of thing that makes me want to go on to the next recipe), and besides, I enjoy the color that the bits of brown skin add to the cake.

HAZELNUT CAKE

Unbleached all-purpose flour	1½ cups (200 g)
Hazelnut meal	¾ cup (90 g)
Baking powder	1½ teaspoons
Fine sea salt	¼ teaspoon
Salted butter	½ cup (110 g), at room temperature
Sugar	1½ cups (300 g)
Vanilla bean	1
Large eggs	2, at room temperature
Heavy cream	¾ cup (210 ml)

HAZELNUT PRALINE TOPPING

Hazelnuts	2 cups (225 g)
Sugar	1 cup (200 g)
Heavy cream	1¼ to 1½ cups (295 to 350 ml)
Flaky sea salt	Pinch

1. Preheat the oven to 350°F (180°C). Lightly butter a 9 × 5-inch (23 × 12-cm) loaf pan. Line the bottom of the pan with parchment paper.

2. **To make the cake:** Whisk the flour, hazelnut meal, baking powder, and salt in a small bowl.

recipe continues ▶

3. Put the butter and sugar in a medium bowl. With the tip of a small knife, split the vanilla bean lengthwise, then scrape the seeds into the bowl, reserving the pod for another use. Beat the mixture with an electric mixer on high speed until it is pale, 4 to 5 minutes.

4. Beat in the eggs, one at a time, beating well after each addition until the mxture is light and fluffy. With the mixer on low speed, add the flour mixture in thirds, alternating with two additions of the cream, and beat, scraping down the sides of the bowl as needed, just until smooth. Spread the batter evenly in the prepared pan.

5. Bake until a wooden toothpick inserted in the center of the cake comes out clean and the top has a nice golden color, 1 hour to 1 hour 10 minutes.

    If the top starts to get too dark, cover it with a sheet of foil.

6. **As soon as the cake is in the oven, start on the topping:** Line a large, rimmed baking sheet with parchment paper.

7. Heat a large skillet over medium heat and add the hazelnuts. Heat the hazelnuts, stirring often, until they are hot, about 3 minutes. Sprinkle in the sugar and let it melt, stirring frequently with a wooden spoon to mix the dry and melted parts. Cook until the nuts are toasted and coated in amber caramel, about 12 minutes.

    Watch the praline carefully to prevent it from burning. It shouldn't get any darker than a rich amber color.

8. Using a lightly oiled silicone spatula, scrape the praline out onto the baking sheet. Let the praline cool completely. Transfer the praline to a chopping board and use a heavy knife to chop it coarsely. Reserve about 2 tablespoons of the chopped glazed hazelnuts.

9. Process about one-fourth of the chopped praline with about ⅓ cup of the cream in a food processor until the mixture is smooth. In three more batches, add more praline and cream and process each time to make a spreadable praline paste. Add the sea salt and pulse to combine.

recipe continues ▸

10. When the cake is done, transfer it to a wire rack and let cool in the pan for 10 minutes. Run a table knife around the inside of the pan to release the cake. Unmold the cake and discard the paper. Turn the cake right side up on the wire rack. Set the rack, with the cake, on a rimmed baking sheet.

11. Spread the praline over the top of the cake and down the sides; you won't need all of it. Sprinkle with the reserved hazelnuts. Let the praline set (it won't get hard) for about 20 minutes. Slice and serve.

CONGRATULATIONS: YOU CAN MAKE NUT BRITTLE

Praline is just a fancy name for old-fashioned nut brittle. You can use this technique with any kind of nut, such as walnuts, pistachios, or almonds. Here are some ways to use this simple confection:

- Crack it into shards to decorate a frosted cake.
- Crush it into small pieces with a mortar and pestle and sprinkle it over ice cream.
- Break it into bite-sized pieces and serve it as a candy with hot coffee after a big dinner when you want a sweet that's not heavy.
- Grind broken-up praline in a food processor and dust it on anything from oatmeal to panna cotta (page 261) for a toasty, nutty sweetness.

ALMOND CAKE

MAKES 10 TO 12 SERVINGS

As children, my brother and I were crazy for almonds and would spend hours using rocks to break open nuts from the trees in our backyard, then beg our mother to turn them into cakes like this one. A sweetened nut paste gives my all-purpose cake batter a completely different texture, look, and profile. The technique sounds a bit tricky—the two cake layers partially bake separately before being combined in one pan with the nut paste sandwiched between them—but if you read through the recipe carefully, you won't have a problem. The flavor is so dreamy; when I take a bite and close my eyes, I can almost feel the rough almond shells and my bruised fingers.

CAKE LAYERS

Unbleached all-purpose flour	1¾ cups (245 g)
Baking powder	1½ teaspoons
Fine sea salt	⅛ teaspoon
Salted butter	½ cup (110 g), at room temperature
Sugar	1½ cups (300 g)
Vanilla bean	1
Large eggs	2, at room temperature
Heavy cream	¾ cup (175 ml)

ALMOND FILLING

Raw almonds	2 cups (200 g)
Sugar	¾ cup (150 g)
Large eggs	2
Fine sea salt	⅛ teaspoon
Heavy cream	3 tablespoons (45 ml)
Lemon	1 (optional)

1. **Make the cake layers:** Preheat the oven to 350°F (180°C). Lightly butter two 9 x 5-inch (23 x 13-cm) loaf pans. Line the bottom of both pans with strips of parchment paper long enough for the ends to hang over both short sides of the pan.

recipe continues ▸

2. Whisk the flour, baking powder, and salt in a small bowl. Put the butter and sugar in a medium bowl. With the tip of a small knife, split the vanilla bean lengthwise, then scrape the seeds into the bowl, saving the pod for another use. Beat the mixture with an electric mixer on high speed until it is pale, 4 to 5 minutes.

3. Beat in the eggs, one at a time, beating well after each addition, until light and fluffy. With the mixer on low speed, add the flour mixture in thirds, alternating with two additions of the cream, and mix, scraping down the sides of the bowl as needed, just until smooth. Divide the batter equally between the two pans and spread it evenly. Bake the cakes until they are deep golden brown and feel just slightly soft (but not wet) when pressed in the center with your fingertip, 20 to 25 minutes.

   Do not overbake the cakes at this stage; they are going to bake again once they've been topped with the filling. If you underbake them, though, the filling will sink into the batter.

4. **While the cakes are baking, make the almond filling:** Grind the almonds and sugar together in a food processor until powdery, about 45 seconds. With the machine running, add the eggs and salt. Slowly pour in the cream, stopping the machine to scrape down the sides with a rubber spatula, and process until the mixture is smooth and thick but spreadable.

5. Remove both cakes from the oven, but leave the oven on. Spread the filling evenly over one cake, gently covering the entire surface. Run a thin knife around the edge of the second cake to loosen it. Using the parchment paper, lift the cake out of the pan and carefully invert it onto the filling-topped cake. Remove the top layer of parchment. Return the combined cake to the oven and bake 20 minutes longer. Set the pan on a wire rack and cool the cake completely.

6. Run a knife around the inside of the pan and invert the cake onto a serving platter over the pan Discard the paper. Cut into slices and grate a bit of lemon zest onto each serving if you like.

GIANT MACARON CAKE

SERVES 10 TO 12

This might be the most unusual way I have put my all-purpose cake batter to use: as the filling rather than the foundation of a multitiered layer cake. We always let our daughters choose what they want for their birthday dessert. When it is Genta's turn, she inevitably chooses something pretty and girly instead of a traditional cake. The year she requested macarons, I thought making one big macaron then turning it into a layer cake by adding cream, cake, and more cream would be fun, and I was right. As it turns out, a giant macaron is faster to make than a bunch of small ones, and it looks really impressive. It's a little messy to serve, but it's still delicious.

MACARON LAYERS

Almond flour	3½ cups (300 g)
Confectioners' sugar	2⅔ cups (300 g)
Baking powder	1 teaspoon
Egg whites	8 large (220 g total)
Red food coloring paste	3 drops, as needed
Granulated sugar	1½ cups (300 g)

CAKE LAYER

Unbleached all-purpose flour	1 cup minus 1 tablespoon (130 g), plus more for pan
Baking powder	¾ teaspoon
Flaky sea salt	⅛ teaspoon
Granulated sugar	¾ cup (150 g)
Salted butter	5 tablespoons (70 g), at room temperature, plus more for pan
Large egg	1, at room temperature
Vanilla bean	1
Heavy cream	7 tablespoons (100 ml)

FRUIT LAYER

Heavy cream	2 cups (475 ml)
Strawberries	1 pound (455 g)
Raspberries	6 ounces (170 g)

recipe continues ▸

1. **Make the macaron layers:** Place a sieve in a large bowl and add the almond flour, confectioners' sugar, and baking powder. Sift the dry ingredients into the bowl, using your fingers to rub the almond flour through the mesh if it is stubborn. Whisk 4 of the egg whites (110 g) with the food coloring in a medium bowl just until the mixture is evenly colored. Set it aside.

   Don't be timid with the food coloring. You want the macaron to be a bright, bold pink.

2. Combine the granulated sugar with ⅓ cup (75 ml) water in a small saucepan. Bring to a boil over high heat, stirring to help dissolve the sugar. Attach a candy thermometer to the pan and cook until the syrup reaches 244°F (118°C), 3 to 5 minutes.

3. While the syrup is cooking, use an electric mixer set on high speed to whip the remaining 4 egg whites (110 g) in a large bowl just until they form soft peaks. Still beating on high, slowly pour a stream of the hot syrup into the bowl—do not pour directly into the beaters, or the syrup will splash. Keep beating on high speed until the eggs whites form stiff, glossy peaks.

4. Let the meringue cool until it is warm but not hot (about 120°F/48°C), which can take about 20 minutes. Add the colored egg whites to the almond flour mixture and use a big rubber spatula to stir them together until blended: Scrape the meringue into the bowl and fold it all together, reaching down to the bottom of the mixture with the spatula and bringing it up and over the rest of the mixture. Turn the bowl one quarter turn and repeat until the mixture is evenly colored but still light and fluffy.

5. Cut 2 sheets of parchment paper. Using a 9-inch (23-cm) round cake pan as a template, draw a circle on each parchment sheet with a dark pencil. Turn the paper over so you can see the circle from the opposite side. Spoon half of the meringue mixture into the center of each circle and use the spatula to spread it evenly toward the edges with a slight dome in the center. Let the shells stand, uncovered, at room temperature for about 1 hour while you make the pound cake.

   Letting the macaron shells stand before you bake them is important! The skin that develops on the surface will keep them from spreading as they bake.

6. **While the macaron layers are standing, make the cake layer:** Preheat the oven to 350°F (180°C), with the oven racks in the top third and center of the oven. Lightly butter a 9 × 2-inch (23 ×5-cm) round cake pan, line the bottom with a parchment paper round.

ONE BATTER, SIX DESSERTS

7. Sift the flour, baking powder, and salt together into a medium bowl. Beat the sugar and butter in another medium bowl with an electric mixer until it is pale, about 3 minutes on high speed. Beat in the eggs, one at a time until light. With the tip of a small knife, split the vanilla bean lengthwise, then scrape the vanilla seeds into the bowl, saving the pod for another use.

8. With the mixer on low speed, add the flour mixture in thirds, alternating with two equal additions of the cream, and beat until smooth. Spread the batter evenly in the pan and sprinkle with flaky salt.

9. Bake on the center rack until the top of the cake is golden brown and springs back when pressed with a fingertip, about 20 minutes. Let the cake cool in the pan on a wire rack for about 10 minutes. Run a knife around the inside of the pan to loosen the cake. Invert and unmold the pan onto the rack and discard the paper. Turn the cake right side up and let cool completely.

10. Now, back to the macaron layers. By this time a thin crust should have formed on the surface. Bake the shells until they feel mostly set underneath the crust, about 30 minutes. Turn off the oven, prop the door open slightly with a wooden spoon, and let them slowly cool and crisp, 45 minutes to 1 hour. Remove from the oven and cool completely.

    The macarons may form browned "feet" around the edges as they bake. You can trim these off if you prefer after they cool.

11. **Make the fruit layer:** Whip the cream in a large bowl with an electric mixer on medium speed until the cream just begins to hold its shape. Hull the strawberries, cut them in half lengthwise, and put in a bowl.

    Do not overwhip the cream—it should barely hold its shape.

12. No more than 30 minutes before you plan to serve the cake, assemble the components. Carefully peel the parchment from one of the macaron shells and place the shell on a cake plate flat side up. Spread it with half of the cream and scatter the strawberries evenly on top. Gently set the pound cake on top. Cover with the remaining cream and the raspberries. Carefully remove the paper from the second macaron, and place it on top of the raspberries, domed side up.

    Use the less perfect of the two macaron shells for the base layer, saving the prettier one for the top. Don't worry if there are cracks, it will still taste great.

13. Let the cake stand for 15 to 20 minutes to slightly soften the meringue. Use a thin, sharp knife to cut into wedges.

"NYC" CHEESECAKE

SERVES 8

I've had a weakness for cheesecake since my first visit to America as a little girl. I tracked down a recipe on the Internet, but it wasn't quite what I remembered. Over time, I've tweaked it to be a bit lighter so I can eat more! Cutting the cream cheese with a bit of mascarpone and yogurt makes the filling incredibly smooth and soft rather than overwhelmingly dense. You could serve this topped with fruit if you want, but honestly, I think it's perfect as is. In fact, the first time René and I went to New York I insisted on going to a diner for a piece of authentic cheesecake, and he said mine was better!

CRUST

Graham crackers	1 package (9 whole cookies) (90 g)
Sugar	3 tablespoons (40 g)
Salted butter	¼ cup (55 g) melted

FILLING

Cream cheese	12 ounces (340g), at room temperature
Plain Greek yogurt	½ cup (120 g)
Mascarpone	½ cup (110 ml), at room temperature
Large eggs	2, at room temperature
Salted butter	1 tablespoon, melted
Vanilla bean	½
Fine sea salt	⅛ teaspoon

1. Preheat the oven to 300°F (150°C).

2. **Make the crust:** Crumble the crackers into a medium bowl and use a pestle or the bottom of a heavy bottle to crush them into fine crumbs. Stir in the sugar. Pour the melted butter over the mixture and stir until very well combined. Press the crumb mixture firmly and evenly into the bottom of a

recipe continues ▶

9-inch springform pan. Bake until the crust looks a little darker and smells sweet and toasty, 10 to 12 minutes.

You can grind the crumbled graham crackers and mix them with the sugar and butter in a food processor if you prefer.

3. **While the crust bakes, make the filling:** Combine the cream cheese with the yogurt and mascarpone in a large bowl. Beat with an electric mixer on medium speed until smooth, scraping down the sides of the bowl as needed. One at a time, beat in the eggs, followed by the melted butter. With a small, sharp knife, split the vanilla bean lengthwise and use the tip of the knife to scrape the seeds into the bowl. Add the salt and mix just until smooth. Do not overbeat the filling.

For a smooth filling, the cream cheese and mascarpone must be at room temperature; set them on the counter an hour or two before you start cooking.

4. Pour the filling into the hot crust and smooth the top. Tap the pan on the counter a few times to release any air bubbles in the filling. Bake until the filling is nearly set in the center, about 26 minutes. Move the cheesecake to a wire rack to cool completely.

The filling will continue to cook even after you take it out of the oven, so don't worry if it doesn't seem completely set. You don't want to let it get brown.

5. When the cheesecake has cooled, cover the pan with plastic wrap and refrigerate until very cold, at least 4 hours or overnight. To serve, run a sharp knife around the inside of the pan to loosen the cheesecake and then remove the sides. Cut the cake into wedges with a thin, sharp knife.

Dip the blade of your knife in cold water and wipe it clean between cuts to keep the slices neat.

PANNA COTTA CARAMEL

SERVES 6

Panna cotta can be rubbery, so I cut back on the gelatin to make sure it comes out soft and silky. The vanilla beans are an important ingredient here and not just for their flavor; the seeds themselves actually add a bit of crunch, so you get tiny little pops in every bite. When you unmold the panna cottas, make sure the water you dip them in is boiling hot. The heat will cause the sides to melt slightly, creating a little bit of sauce and releasing them from the cup, and I'm convinced it also subtly changes the texture. At home I would serve this sprinkled with a bit of powdered licorice, which is really popular in Denmark (try it sometime; you'll be amazed how good it is), but you can pair it with berries or nothing at all. You will need six small ramekins or custard cups to make these.

Sugar	¾ cup (75 g)
Unflavored gelatin powder	1¾ teaspoons
Heavy cream	2 cups (480 ml)
Vanilla bean	1

1. Arrange six ½-cup/120-ml–capacity ramekins or custard cups on your counter. Stir the sugar and 2 tablespoons water together in a small, heavy saucepan over high heat until boiling. Stop stirring and let the mixture boil, occasionally swirling the saucepan, until the caramel is dark amber, about 3 minutes. Immediately pour the caramel into the ramekins and swirl each to coat the bottom with the caramel.

   The caramel will harden when it hits the cold ramekins, so work quickly.

2. Pour 2 tablespoons water into a small bowl. Stir in the gelatin and let stand until the gelatin has absorbed the water.

3. Pour the cream into a medium saucepan. Split the vanilla bean lengthwise and use the tip of a small knife to scrape the seeds into the pan, and add the pod to the saucepan, too. Bring to a simmer over medium heat, stirring almost constantly. Reduce the heat to very low. Whisk the softened gelatin mixture

recipe continues ▸

into the hot cream and whisk until it is completely dissolved, 1 to 2 minutes. Remove from the heat and discard the pod.

Stir the gelatin very well to be sure it dissolves entirely. Adjust the heat as needed so the mixture doesn't come to a simmer.

4. Pour the cream mixture into a liquid measuring cup with a spout, then divide the mixture among the ramekins.

5. Loosely cover each one with plastic wrap. Refrigerate the panna cottas until they are chilled and set, at least 4 hours or overnight.

6. To serve, bring a kettle of water to a boil. Uncover the panna cottas. Pour about 1 inch (2.5 cm) of boiling water into a small bowl. One at a time, set the ramekins in the hot water until the panna cotta is easily loosened and starts to melt a bit around the edges, 10 to 20 seconds; don't let any water slosh inside the ramekin.

Replace the water in the bowl if it cools down. You want it really hot.

7. Place a dessert plate over the ramekin. Holding the ramekin and plate together, invert and unmold. Repeat with the remaining ramekins.

VANILLA BEAN ICE CREAM

SERVES 6 TO 8; MAKES 1¼ QUARTS (1.2 L)

Most store-bought vanilla ice cream doesn't even really taste like vanilla, a flavor I adore, so when I developed this recipe I added so many vanilla seeds the end product was almost gray! You may be surprised at how little added sugar there is in this recipe, but I find fresh organic cream inherently quite sweet. Try it my way once; I'll bet you would never know that it doesn't have much sugar. Fresh vanilla beans are a splurge, for sure, but you can use the scraped pods to flavor sugar, custards, or vodka or make the apple recipe on page 229. When I see vanilla beans on sale I stock up, stashing them in the freezer until needed. I prefer Tahitian vanilla beans because they have a very rich, perfumed aroma, but the standard Madagascar Bourbon beans work, too. You don't need a fancy ice cream maker for this; one with a removable freezer canister works fine. I just store mine in the freezer (usually with a bag of frozen peas inside!).

Large egg yolks	9
Sugar	½ cup (100 g)
Vanilla beans	2
Heavy cream	2 cups (480 ml)
Whole milk	1 cup (240 ml)
Fine sea salt	Pinch

1. Put the egg yolks and sugar in a medium heatproof bowl. Split the vanilla beans lengthwise and use the tip of a small knife to scrape the seeds into the bowl; set the pods aside. Whisk well until the mixture is pale yellow and almost doubled in volume.

2. Heat the cream, milk, and scraped vanilla pods in a medium, heavy-bottomed saucepan over medium heat until the mixture is hot but not simmering. Remove from the heat and let the cream mixture steep for 15 minutes. Gradually whisk the hot cream mixture into the egg yolk mixture, then pour this custard back into the saucepan. Stir in the salt.

3. Place a sieve over a medium bowl near the stove. Cook the custard over low heat, stirring constantly with a silicone or wooden spatula, until it is

recipe continues ▸

CONGRATULATIONS: YOU CAN MAKE CRÈME ANGLAISE

The base for vanilla ice cream is actually a classic dessert sauce known as crème anglaise. Make it exactly as for the ice cream, but instead of freezing it, strain and refrigerate until chilled, at least 4 hours. This recipe makes about 3½ cups (840 ml) of the sauce; halve the recipe, if you wish. You can serve this as a sauce for many desserts, especially plain cakes like the Almond Cake on page 251 or Plum Cake on page 241.

thickened and steaming but not boiling. To see if it's thick enough, draw your fingertip through the custard on the spatula—it should cut a swath through the custard. If the custard starts to simmer, immediately remove it from the heat. Strain the custard through the sieve into the bowl and discard the vanilla pods.

4. Let the custard cool to room temperature. Cover tightly with plastic wrap and refrigerate until chilled, at least 4 hours or overnight.

   If you want to speed up the chilling, put the custard in a metal bowl and place it in a large bowl of iced water, stirring often. It will be cold in about 30 minutes.

5. Transfer the chilled custard to the ice cream maker. Freeze the ice cream according to the manufacturer's directions. Transfer to a covered container and place in the freezer until firm enough to scoop, at least 3 hours or overnight.

   Don't worry if the ice cream seems too soft when it comes out of the ice cream maker; it will get firmer in the freezer.

CONGRATULATIONS: YOU CAN MAKE ICE CREAM

Consider this basic vanilla custard your canvas for improvisation and vary it with flavorings or add-ins. It's easy to create other flavors:

- For spice-flavored ice cream, delete the vanilla beans. Use 2 cinnamon sticks, 2 tablespoons allspice berries, 1 tablespoon whole cloves, or a combination.
- For fruit ice cream, use 1 vanilla bean. Before churning the custard, add a handful or two of your favorite freeze-dried fruit, such as raspberries or strawberries. Don't use fresh fruit; it contains too much moisture and will make crystals in the ice cream.
- For chunky ice cream, just before you take the ice cream out of the machine, toss in any of the following: brownie bits, chocolate chips, chunks of chocolate dough, small balls of marzipan, or raisins soaked in rum (drain them before adding).

SUGAR-CURED EGG YOLK
IN A MERINGUE CLOUD

SERVES 4

Considering that this dessert is essentially just eggs and sugar, it's amazing how many different textures are in every bite. It combines crisp baked meringue and soft, fluffy uncooked meringue, topped with a delicate sugar-cured egg yolk that makes its own delicious sauce. I won't pretend this is a fast and easy dessert, but it is nice after a relaxed weekend meal when you want something impressive but not too rich or heavy. Consider it a master class in making meringue. Because they are not cooked, you may want to use pasteurized eggs for this if you are not completely confident about their safety. It's also a good idea to make an extra yolk or two as insurance against breakage later. If you do, however, save the extra whites for another use.

Large eggs	4
Sugar	1¼ cups (250 g)
Heavy cream	1 cup (240 ml)
Freeze-dried raspberries	About 24

1. Preheat the oven to 200°F (100°C). Line a large, rimmed baking sheet with parchment paper.

2. **Make the crisp meringue:** Separate two of the eggs, collecting the whites in a medium bowl and setting the yolks aside in another bowl. Cover the yolks and refrigerate.

   Be sure not to get even a drop of yolk in the whites or they won't beat properly. Use the edge of a broken shell to scoop out any stray yolk.

3. Add about 1 inch (2.5 cm) hot water to a large bowl. Place the bowl of egg whites in the water and stir just until the whites lose their chill (use your finger to check), 30 seconds to 1 minute. Using an electric mixer on high speed, beat the egg whites until they are very foamy. Now, gradually beat in

recipe continues ▸

½ cup (100 g) of the sugar and beat until the meringue forms soft, shiny peaks and sticks to the sides of the bowl.

Do not overbeat the meringue. If it starts to look grainy or separated, throw it out and start over.

4. Using a spoon, spread the meringue into a layer about ¼ inch (6 mm) thick on the prepared baking sheet. It is going to be crumbled later, so it doesn't need to be even or smooth. Bake the meringue until crisp, 1½ to 2 hours. Turn off the oven, prop the oven door slightly ajar with a wooden spoon, and let the meringue cool completely on the baking sheet.

The meringue will be slightly soft when you turn off the oven but will crisp as it cools.

5. About 2 hours before serving, bring 1 quart (960 ml) water and ¼ cup (50 g) of the sugar to a boil in a medium saucepan over high heat, stirring to dissolve the sugar. Remove from the heat and pour the liquid into a heatproof bowl. Separate the remaining 2 eggs, putting the whites in a clean medium bowl. Carefully add the yolks as well as the 2 refrigerated yolks to the syrup. Let them stand in the syrup for 1½ to 2 hours at room temperature.

6. To serve, whip the remaining egg whites with a whisk or an electric mixer on high speed until they form soft peaks. Gradually add the remaining ½ cup (100 g) sugar and continue whipping until the meringue forms stiff, glossy peaks and sticks to the sides of the bowl. Once again, be careful not to overbeat the whites.

7. Coarsely crumble the baked meringues into 4 serving bowls. Add a dollop of soft meringue to each bowl, mounding it lightly. Using the back of a spoon, make a small indentation in each mound. Carefully cup your hand and scoop out a yolk one at a time, letting the syrup drip back into the bowl and adding a yolk to each indentation. Divide the cream among the bowls, pouring it around but not over the soft meringue. Use your fingers to crush the dried raspberries to a coarse powder and sprinkle it over the yolks. Serve immediately.

FROZEN AVOCADO CAKE

SERVES 12 TO 14

Here's another example of how basic building blocks like a crumb crust and a sweetened cream cheese filling can be combined for very different results. This may sound a lot like the "NYC" cheesecake on page 258, but it is a lighter, more refreshing dessert akin to an ice cream cake. Adding sweetened condensed milk to the crust gives it a candy-like texture that reminds me of a Twix bar (a childhood weakness I rarely get to indulge since marrying a chef!). That same sweetness accentuates the buttery quality of ripe avocados. Chill it thoroughly, then let the cake sit at room temperature for a bit before you slice it. It's so refreshing on a hot day.

Softened butter	For the pan
Graham crackers	8 whole crackers (120 g)
Digestive biscuits or 4 additional graham crackers	11 cookies (60 g)
Condensed milk	2 (14-ounce/397-g) cans
Hass avocados	3
Cream cheese	1 pound (455 g), at room temperature
Fine sea salt	Pinch
Lemon	2
Limes	2

1. Preheat the oven to 350°F (180°C). Lightly butter the inside of a 9-inch (23-cm) springform pan.

2. **Make the crust:** Crumble the crackers and cookies into a medium bowl. Use a pestle or the bottom of a heavy bottle to crush them into fine crumbs. Add ⅓ cup (75 ml) of the condensed milk and stir until very well combined. Press the crumb mixture firmly and evenly into the bottom of the pan. Bake until the crust looks a little darker and smells sweet and toasty, 12 to 15 minutes. Cool the crust in the pan on a wire rack.

   You can grind the crumbled graham crackers and mix them with the sugar and condensed milk in a food processor if you prefer.

recipe continues ▸

3. One at a time, cut an avocado in half lengthwise. Twist the halves to separate them. Hold the half with the pit in one hand. Holding the knife in your other hand, rap the knife blade into the pit to lodge it there. Twist the knife to loosen and remove the pit. Use a large spoon to scoop the avocado flesh onto a chopping board, discarding the skins. Coarsely chop the avocados.

4. Add the chopped avocados, cream cheese, remaining condensed milk, and salt to a food processor. Grate the zest of 1 lemon and set aside. Squeeze the zested lemon and the limes (you should have about ⅓ cup/75 ml lemon), reserving the remaining lemon for garnish. Add the juice to the avocados and process the mixture until smooth, scraping down the sides of the bowl as needed.

   You can combine the filling in a blender instead but you may need to work in batches.

5. Spread the filling in the cooled crust and sprinkle with the grated lemon zest. Cover the pan and freeze until the filling is firm, at least 6 hours or preferably overnight.

6. Let the frozen cake stand at room temperature for 15 to 30 minutes before slicing. Dipping a thin knife into hot water between each cut, slice the cake into wedges and serve, topping each serving with freshly grated lemon zest.

MY TIRAMISÙ

SERVES 8 TO 10

One of my favorite dessert building blocks, a crisp crumb crust, shows up in this unconventional tiramisù. The slightly salty, sweet layer at the bottom adds substance and some nice crunch to a dish that can be on the soft and mushy side. I flavor the coffee for dipping the ladyfingers with a combination of almond liqueur such as Amaretto and rum or Armagnac because I like the way the liqueur's sweetness mellows the sharper edge of the rum, but if you don't have both, just increase the amount of rum or Armagnac. It has a digestive quality that is good with a dessert this rich. You'll get the best crunch from the crust the day this is made, but even when it softens, it's still tasty.

CRUST

Salted butter	6 tablespoons (82 g), melted, plus more for the pan
Graham crackers	12 whole crackers (180 g)
Sugar	2 tablespoons
Fine sea salt	Pinch

FILLING

Large eggs	3
Mascarpone	3½ cups (785 ml)
Heavy cream	⅔ cup (150 ml)
Sugar	½ cup (100 g)
Vanilla bean	1
Brewed French roast coffee	2½ cups (600 ml), cooled
Almond liqueur such as Amaretto	3 tablespoons (45 ml)
Rum or Armagnac	2 tablespoons
Italian ladyfingers *(savioardi)*	About 36
Unsweetened cocoa powder	2 tablespoons
Bittersweet chocolate	1 (3.5-ounce/100-g) bar (about 70 percent cacao)

1. Preheat the oven to 300°F (150°C). Lightly butter an 9 × 13-inch (23 × 33-cm) baking pan.

recipe continues ▸

2. **Make the crust:** Crumble the crackers into a medium bowl and use a pestle or the bottom of a wine bottle to crush them into fine crumbs. Combine the crumbs, sugar and salt. Stir in the melted butter and mix until combined. Press the crumb mixture firmly and evenly into the bottom of the pan. Bake until the bottom looks a little darker and smells sweet and toasty, about 5 minutes.

   You can also crumble the crackers into a food processor and process them.

3. **Make the filling:** Separate the eggs, putting the yolks and whites into separate medium bowls. Add the mascarpone, cream, and sugar to the yolks and whisk until smooth and combined. Using a small, sharp knife, split the vanilla bean lengthwise then use the tip of the knife to scrape the seeds into the mascarpone mixture, saving the pod for another use. Whisk again.

4. Whip the egg whites with a clean whisk or an electric mixer on high speed until medium-stiff peaks form. Using a rubber spatula, stir about one-fourth of the whites into the mascarpone mixture to lighten it, then fold in the remaining whites.

   Folding in the egg whites keeps them light. Use a spatula to cut down and through the mixture, bringing up the batter at the bottom of the bowl. Give the bowl a quarter turn and repeat until the batter is almost uniform in color.

5. Mix the coffee, almond liqueur, and rum in a wide, shallow bowl. Spread a very thin layer of the mascarpone cream over the cooled crust. One at a time, dip the ladyfingers into the coffee mixture, submerging them completely, then arrange them on the mascarpone, placing them closely together and using about half the ladyfingers per layer (break them to fit if necessary). Spread half of the remaining mascarpone cream over the ladyfingers in an even layer and sift 1½ tablespoons of the cocoa powder on top. Repeat with the remaining ladyfingers, mascarpone cream, and cocoa.

   Be careful to soak the ladyfingers just briefly or they will fall apart.

6. Cover and refrigerate until chilled, at least 3 hours or overnight. Just before serving use a vegetable peeler to shave chocolate onto the tiramisù. (You will not need all of the chocolate.)

   If the chocolate is close to body temperature, it will curl when you shave it. If cool, it will make shreds. Both look good.

CHOCOLATE CHUNK COOKIES

MAKES 2½ DOZEN COOKIES

I've never liked the look of cookies made with chopped nuts because they make the surface so lumpy and uneven; using almond flour gives you the same nutty richness in every bite, with a smooth top. I tried making these cookies without any wheat flour at all, but in the end I decided this blend gave the best results. Chop up a nice dark chocolate bar rather than using chocolate chips for this if you can so every bite is a little different (although a combination of bittersweet chips and chunks does the job, too). One of the nice things about these cookies is that you don't have to chill the dough before baking them, and depending on how long you cook them they bake up chewy or crisp, as you prefer.

Salted butter	⅔ cup (145 g), at room temperature
Granulated sugar	⅔ cup (135 g)
Dark brown sugar	⅔ cup (135 g) packed
Vanilla bean	1
Large eggs	2, at room temperature
Almond flour or almond meal	1½ cups (140 g)
Unbleached all-purpose flour	¾ cup (100 g)
Baking powder	1 teaspoon
Baking soda	½ teaspoon baking soda
Salt	½ teaspoon
Bittersweet chocolate	7 ounces (200 g)

1. Preheat the oven to 350°F (180°C), with the oven racks in the center and top third of the oven. Line two baking sheets with parchment paper.

2. Mix the butter, granulated sugar, and brown sugar in a large bowl with an electric mixer on high speed until the mixture is light in color and creamy, about 2 minutes, scraping down the sides of the bowl toward the center as needed. With a small, sharp knife, split the vanilla bean lengthwise, then scrape the seeds into the batter, saving the pod for another use.

recipe continues ▸

3. Beat in the eggs one at a time, beating well after each addition.

4. Whisk the almond flour, all-purpose flour, baking powder, baking soda, and salt together in a small bowl. With the mixer on low speed, gradually mix in the flour mixture. Coarsely chop the chocolate into ½-inch (12-cm) pieces (they do not have to be uniform) and mix them into the dough.

   Almond flour is made from skinless, or blanched, almonds, almond meal from almonds with the skins on. You'll get a paler cookie from the flour, but it tends to cost a little more.

5. Using about 1 tablespoonful for each cookie, drop the dough onto the baking sheets, about 2 inches (5 cm) apart. Bake for about 15 minutes, switching the baking sheets from top to bottom halfway through baking, until the edges are crispy but the center is still soft and chewy.

   You can bake these as long as 17 minutes if you like your cookies very crisp, but I pull them out after 12 or 13 minutes so they are soft and chewy and just barely crisp around the edges.

6. Let the cookies cool on the baking sheets for about 5 minutes. Serve them warm or cool to room temperature. The cookies can be stored in an airtight container for up to 5 days.

BROWNIES WITH FLAKY SALT
AND WHITE CHOCOLATE CHUNKS

MAKES 12 TO 15 BROWNIES

The world is divided between those who like their brownies cakey and those who like them chewy. If you are in the latter camp: you're welcome! These are dense and chocolatey, and while you can eat them as soon as they are made, they are even better when refrigerated overnight, which makes them extra chewy and fudgy. I sometimes stick them in the freezer for 30 minutes after cutting them into bars because I like the chocolate/caramel bar texture that develops. I always make them with Valrhona Caraibe, which is 66 percent cacao. You can use another brand that you like, but I find I get the best results with chocolate that has a cacao content of 60 to 70 percent. Save your super-bittersweet bars for late-night snacking. White chocolate chips will work for this, but I prefer the irregular appearance you get when you chop a bar into bits.

Bittersweet chocolate	7 ounces (200 g) (60 to 70 percent cacao)
Salted butter	½ cup (110 grams)
Sugar	Generous 1 cup (200 g)
Large eggs	2, at room temperature
Vanilla bean	1
Unbleached all-purpose flour	Generous ½ cup (75 g)
Baking powder	1 teaspoon
Fine sea salt	¼ teaspoon
White chocolate	3½ ounces (100 g)
Flaky sea salt	¼ to ½ teaspoon

1. Preheat the oven to 350°F (180°C). Cut a 9 × 16-inch (23 × 40.5-cm) strip of parchment paper and use it to line the bottom and two sides of a 9-inch (23-cm) square pan, letting the excess paper hang over the ends.

   Don't trim the parchment to fit the bottom of the pan. You will need the overhang to lift the brownies out of the pan once they cool.

recipe continues ▸

2. Bring about 1 inch (2.5 cm) water to a boil in a medium saucepan over high heat. Turn the heat to low so the water is barely simmering. Place a glass or metal bowl over the pan.

   The bottom of the bowl shouldn't touch the simmering water. If the chocolate gets too hot, it can become grainy.

3. Coarsely chop the chocolate and put it in the bowl. As it starts to melt, cut the butter into chunks and add them to the bowl. Let them melt together, stirring occasionally. Remove the bowl from the saucepan and let the chocolate mixture cool for about 5 minutes.

   If the chocolate mixture is too hot, it will scramble the beaten eggs in the next step.

4. Combine the sugar and eggs in a medium bowl and beat with an electric mixer on high speed until pale and light in texture, about 2 minutes. Use the tip of a small knife to split the vanilla bean lengthwise and scrape the seeds into the egg mixture, saving the pod for another use.

5. Add the chocolate mixture and mix on low speed until thoroughly incorporated. Sift the flour, baking powder, and sea salt onto the chocolate mixture and mix by hand just until combined. Coarsely chop the white chocolate into small bits and fold them into the batter.

   You don't want to overmix the batter after adding the dry ingredients or the brownies will be tough; mix just until it is a uniform dark brown.

6. Spread the batter in the prepared pan. Sprinkle with flaky salt to taste. Bake the brownies until a wooden toothpick inserted in the center comes out with just a few moist crumbs, 25 to 30 minutes. Don't overbake! Place the pan on a wire rack to cool completely.

7. Run a knife around the inside of the pan and lift up on the paper flaps to remove the brownie from the pan in one piece. Let the brownies cool completely before cutting into bars, and store in the refrigerator. Serve cold or at room temperature.

WALNUT CRESCENTS

MAKES ABOUT 3 DOZEN COOKIES

Talk about old-fashioned! The basic recipe for these cookies came to my mother from an American friend who said it had been in her family for generations. That must be true, because it's so simple you can literally make it by hand, just squeezing and rubbing the ingredients together with your fingers (be sure to remove your rings and jewelry if you try this). If you are not a fan of walnuts, substitute pecans, macadamia nuts, hazelnuts, or even a combination, especially if you find yourself with odds and ends in your baking cabinet. This is a perfect recipe to make with the kids, and they love rolling and shaping the crescents. If you wish, sift confectioners' sugar over the warm cookies—don't try to roll them in the sugar, they are too delicate.

Walnut pieces or halves	2 cups (225 g)
Unbleached all-purpose flour	2 cups (280 g)
Fine sea salt	¼ teaspoon
Salted butter	1 cup (225 g), at room temperature
Sugar	½ cup (100 g)
Vanilla bean	1

1. Preheat the oven to 350°F (180°C), with the oven racks in the center and top third of the oven. Line two large rimmed baking sheets with parchment paper or silicone baking mats.

2. Grind the walnuts in a food processor with ½ cup (65 g) of the flour until powdery. Add the remaining flour with the salt and pulse to combine.

3. Put the butter and sugar in a medium bowl. Split the vanilla bean lengthwise and use the tip of a knife to scrape the seeds into the bowl, saving the pod for another use. Mix with an electric mixer set on high speed until the mixture is pale and light in texture, about 2 minutes. With the mixer on low speed, gradually add the flour mixture until the dough comes together.

   The dough may seem crumbly, but it will hold together when you shape the cookies.

recipe continues ▸

4. Using about 1 tablespoon for each cookie, squeeze the dough into a rough log, then roll it back and forth on your work surface to make a smoother log about 2 inches (5 cm) long and slightly tapered at each end. Gently bend the log into a crescent and place on the baking sheet. Repeat with the remaining dough. The cookies can be placed fairly close together because they don't spread much as they bake, but don't let them touch.

5. Bake, switching the positions of the baking sheets from top to bottom halfway through baking, until the cookies are very lightly browned around the edges, about 20 minutes. Let the cookies cool completely on the baking sheet. Store in an airtight container at room temperature for about 5 days.

The cookies are fragile while hot, so don't move them off the baking sheet too soon.

WALNUT SQUARES

SERVES 12

René is not big on sweets, but he is obsessed with nuts, especially walnuts, so I knew they were the key to making a cake he would love. Although it contains very little sugar and almost no flour, there's a lot happening with this cake: it's moist, dense, and has great texture. Walnuts are so oily that the cake, though plain, has an enormous amount of flavor and also keeps very well. I made this for the editors of Bon Appétit *when they came to our house for a shoot, and they ended up liking it so much they named it one of the best recipes of the year. It's filling, so serve it in small pieces.*

Raw sugar (turbinado)	6 tablespoons (75 g)
Walnut halves and pieces	7 cups (795 g)
Unbleached all-purpose flour	¾ cup (105 g)
Almond flour	1½ cups (135 g)
Fine sea salt	1 teaspoon
Salted butter	1 cup (225 g), at room temperature, plus more for the pan
Granulated sugar	¾ cup (150 g)
Large eggs	6, at room temperature
Heavy cream	¾ cup (180 ml)
Plain yogurt	½ cup (120 ml), preferably whole milk or low-fat (not nonfat)
Vanilla bean	

TOPPING

Heavy cream	2 cups (480 ml), for serving

1. Preheat oven to 350°F (180°C). Lightly butter a 9 × 13-inch (23 × 33-cm) baking pan. Sprinkle 3 tablespoons of the sugar in the bottom of the pan.

2. Pulse 2 cups (225 g) of the walnuts in the food processor until they are coarsely chopped. Transfer the chopped walnuts to a bowl and set aside.

recipe continues ▸

3. Add the remaining 5 cups (560 g) walnuts to the food processor with the flour. Working in two batches if necessary, process until the mixture is very finely chopped and powdery. Add the almond flour and salt and pulse to combine. Set the walnut flour mixture aside.

   Adding the all-purpose flour to the walnuts keeps the nuts from becoming an oily paste.

4. Put the butter and granulated sugar in a medium bowl. Use the tip of a small knife to split the vanilla bean lengthwise, then scrape the seeds into the bowl, saving the pod for another use. Beat the mixture with an electric mixer set on high speed until it is light in color and texture, about 3 minutes. One at a time, beat in the eggs, beating well after each addition.

5. Reduce the mixer speed to low. Mix in about one-third of the walnut flour mixture, followed by the heavy cream, scraping down the bowl as needed. Mix in another third of the walnut flour mixture, followed by the yogurt. Mix in the remaining walnut flour mixture and beat, scraping down the bowl as needed, just until smooth. Using the spatula, gently fold in the walnuts. Do not overmix.

6. Spread the batter evenly in the pan and sprinkle with the remaining 3 tablespoons sugar. Bake until the top is golden brown and a wooden toothpick or fork comes out clean, 50 to 60 minutes. Set the pan on a wire rack to cool completely.

7. When ready to serve, whip the cream in a large bowl with an electric mixer set on high speed just until the cream forms soft peaks. Cut the cake into squares and serve with the whipped cream.

COCONUT TOPS

MAKES 12 TO 14

It should be obvious by now that we are a family that eats a lot of eggs and I often have yolks or whites in the fridge, depending on what I've made the day before. Since I never want to throw anything out, I'm always looking for ways to use them. This is the ideal way to use up extra egg whites when I've made mayo or cured eggs. Less a dessert than a confection and similar to American macaroons, these sweet and sticky little treats come together in just minutes. As an added bonus, they are gluten-free. You can gussy up the chocolate with chopped nuts or crushed freeze-dried berries before they set.

Desiccated coconut	2⅔ cups (260 g), or more as needed
Brown sugar	⅔ cup (130 g) packed
Granulated sugar	⅔ cup (130 g)
Large egg whites	4
Semisweet or bittersweet chocolate	5 ounces (140 g)
Flaky sea salt	1 teaspoon, or to taste

1. Preheat the oven to 350°F (180°C). Line a large, rimmed baking sheet with parchment paper.

2. Cook the coconut, brown sugar, granulated sugar, and egg whites in a medium saucepan over medium heat, stirring constantly, just until the sugars have melted. If the mixture is too runny to shape by the spoonful, add more coconut.

3. Using two soup spoons, drop heaping tablespoonfuls of the coconut mixture onto the prepared baking sheet, spacing them about 2 inches (5 cm) apart. They do not have to be perfect, but try to make them about the same size.

4. Bake until the coconut mounds are golden brown, 18 to 20 minutes. Let stand on the baking sheets until completely cool.

recipe continues ▸

5. Bring about 1 inch (2.5 cm) water to a boil in a medium saucepan over high heat. Turn the heat to low so the water is barely simmering. Place a glass or metal bowl over the pan. Coarsely chop the chocolate and put in the bowl. Let the chocolate melt, stirring occasionally, until it is almost, but not completely, melted. Remove the bowl from the saucepan and let the chocolate stand, stirring often, until fully melted and slightly cooled and thickened.

    The bottom of the bowl shouldn't touch the simmering water as the chocolate melts. If the chocolate gets too hot, it can become grainy.

6. One at a time, dip the bottom of each cookie into the chocolate, just so the chocolate comes about ⅛ inch (3 mm) up the sides of the cookie. Transfer the cookies to a plate, chocolate side up. Before the chocolate sets, sprinkle with the salt. Refrigerate the cookies until the chocolate hardens, about 15 minutes, then turn them upright and cover with plastic wrap or transfer to a covered container. Store in the refrigerator, but serve at room temperature.

    Sprinkle chopped nuts or ground freeze-dried berries over the chocolate just after dipping them in the melted chocolate, if you like.

ACKNOWLEDGMENTS

Thank you to my wonderful family, friends, recipe testers, and everyone who has been a part of making this book.

Pam Krauss

Kim Witherspoon

Sandi Mendelson

Ditte Isager

Ashley Tucker

Christine Rudolf

Gabe Ulla

Jan Rasmussen

Jeff Gordinier

Daniel Patterson

David Chang

Frank Castronovo

Frank Falcinelli

Bente Svendsen

Annika de las Herras

Josefine Sofia Svendsen

Mads Sig Thøger Møller

Mikkel westergaard

Arve krognes

Veronika Arverelo Rosforth

Sune Rosforth

Hannah Parker

Patricia Tind Jørgensen

Jakob Block

Bente Svendsen

Meeka Kameoka Livingston

Carine Høgsberg plath

Niels plath

Mathilde Kjær Hansen

Julie Kerzel Duel

David Affertsholt-Allen

Denise Boelmann

Nora Langseth Hansø

Henning Michel

Micala Bendix

The Early Years in Portugal

As far back as I can remember, I have loved to eat. I was born in Portugal in 1985. My parents were penniless musicians: my mother was born in a tiny Danish village and my father came from London. They met in Paris while my mother was an *au pair* and my father was making whatever money he could as a street musician in the Latin Quarter.

They had my brother, Marcus, not too long after they met. He was born while they were living on a campsite in Saint-Tropez. Six months out of the year, they would travel the country, busking around, until 1984, when my paternal grandfather bought the three of them a small home in a Portuguese village called Boutoque, not far from Tavira.

I only spent my early years in Portugal, so I don't remember everything about the experience perfectly. But some vivid memories, both dark and beautiful, have stuck with me. On the more somber end, I can easily remember how my dad acquired a very strong taste for alcohol. His mood would change for seemingly no reason, and he was hard on my mother. He never took it out on my brother and I directly. But whenever we had to deal with any of these episodes, my brother would cover my eyes and sing to me. He'd tell me that everything would be okay and that it would be over soon.

I would spend most days with my mother, since my brother had school and my father was at the bar. The house came with two hectares of land on which my mother grew as many different fruits and vegetables as possible. It already had some pretty amazing trees on it: olive, fig, orange, pomegranate, almond, and walnut among them.

My good, warm memories from this time are all connected to food.

I would walk around the garden picking, touching, smelling, and tasting the various plants. During one of my early explorations, I found a bush with what looked like light-green peas on it. I tasted them—they had a sweet flavor, so I ate lots and lots. I then showed them to my mother. I remember the look on her face, thinking I had just eaten something poisonous. She forced her fingers down my throat to make me vomit. It was horrible, but after that, I learned to master the area. She often reminds me that I learned to identify all the varieties and that she would ask me to go fetch certain things for her throughout the day.

One of my favorite bits of the land was a patch of poppies. I would lie in the middle of it. It was my little secret world. When I was there, alone, I felt like a princess from one of my fairy-tale books.

We had chickens, geese, a donkey, chameleons, sheep, goats, several cats, and a dog. Every once in a while, my parents would buy a whole pig, and the men of the village would hang it, let it bleed out, and then butcher it. The wives taught my mother what to do with every bit of the animal—down to the blood.

But my clearest memory from Portugal was being able to eat pomegranates right off the tree, warm from the sun. I can still feel the light hitting the top of my head and back of my neck, the sticky, sweet liquid running down my chin and arms, and the resinous taste from the peel that I was too impatient to ever deal with properly. I hated its bitter taste, but the flavor of the actual fruit was amazing. Picking out the fragile seeds within was a favorite ritual. When I managed to get one out without damaging it, I would kind of admire it for a second, holding it up toward the sun, which would reveal the little tiny seed in the middle of the beautiful pink pearl. I would then put it between my teeth, bite down, and feel it burst into my mouth.

One of our neighbors would always come by with buckets of the ripest, plumpest tomatoes. When she arrived, I'd instantly take a seat on the ground and eat her offerings as she and my mother chatted. Their voices would fade into a blur as I sat right there on the ground devouring the tomatoes, the juice and seeds bursting out of the fruit.

My brother was great to me. He was patient with me and never showed any signs of being annoyed about having to take care of his little sister. One of the things we would do together was gather almonds. We would sit on the steps of the house cracking them. I'd have to use a large rock, since my brother never let me have the one ham-

mer we had in the house. On some unfortunate occasions, that rock would also catch one of my fingers. The pain was all worth it, since cracking open those almonds meant that my mother could make her stunning almond and marzipan cake—a recipe she came up with so that none of the nuts that grew on the tree went to waste.

Moving to the City, and the Perfect Chicken

When I was around four, we went to London to see my paternal grandparents and ended up staying there for seven months. After that, my parents went their separate ways and my mother, my brother, and I moved to Denmark.

I don't really have any memories—not even food memories—from those first years in Scandinavia. The first four years, Mom trained to become a pedagogue, working with children in need. When she was done with her studies, she went on to help young refugees from Somalia. She'd pull late-night shifts, often going a full twenty-four hours. Yet she'd still make food for us whenever possible.

Eventually I started standing on a chair in the kitchen making porridge for myself. I would stir it and wait patiently for it to begin to bubble. Those hot spheres of air that would disappeared and reappeared on the surface were lots of fun to look at. I'd sometimes play a game with myself, trying to guess where the next slow, lazy air pocket would appear.

I graduated from porridge to whisking together omelets and scrambled eggs. I'd throw in everything I could from the fridge, as well as way too many dried herbs. I started picking up tricks and bits of information all by myself. I learned that when

I would put chopped tomatoes into the whisked eggs, it would ruin the scramble. I hadn't taken the seeds out of the tomatoes, which would water out the whole thing on the frying pan—you could tell from the completely fluorescent liquid that would run out to the sides.

I enjoyed all of this as a hobby, but it became a necessity since my mom's job was so demanding, and my big brother, being completely confident that I could take care of myself, would often go out or to a friend's house instead of cooking us dinner. So I tried to learn to cook as many things as possible.

One of the first big steps was roasted chicken, my favorite. One day I persuaded Mom to let me rub the chicken with oil and salt. I remember the tickling sensation of the salt under my hands and between my fingers, and the strangeness of the cold chicken skin. It was a new feeling, and it was nice: I had the sense that I was making something grown-up. I was making real dinner. I turned on the oven and placed the chicken in a roasting pan. I watched the whole cooking process, making sure it achieved just the right level of crispiness—that golden, glowing color.

By the time I was seven, I could make the perfect vinaigrette. I'd whip that up every single day to dress the green salad that was always on our table at dinner. That was one of the things Mom carried over from her days working as a nanny in Paris. She slowly let me have total freedom in the kitchen. The only condition was that I return things to a fairly decent state when I was through. I usually would have to do the dishes every day, but when I cooked dinner for us, Mom would do them. I loved that. It made me feel very big.

Learning to Improvise

In my adolescent years, I started watching food programs obsessively. I'd take notes. This was one of the greatest parts of staying home sick from school. It all really started when I was struck with mono. It was just so, so boring. I'd usually be stuck watching *Days of Our Lives* marathons, but it got to the point where I just had to flip through the channels. One day, I landed on *Ready, Steady, Cook*, with Ainsley Harriott, which became an instant favorite. A three-course meal in twenty minutes? Perfect. Right after Harriott came Antonio Carluccio visiting a family in the Italian countryside—people who would make sausage from scratch, mixing in all kinds of herbs and garlic. It made my mouth water. After that episode came more Carluccio. This time, he made a beautiful pasta sauce with mussels, tomatoes, garlic, capers, and herbs. I could almost smell the sauce in the pan and taste the acidity of the capers, cutting through it all. I didn't even like capers! But the way he was making the dish, it all made sense. It made me hungry for the first time in a week. I even drooled a bit.

When the program was over, I quickly wrote it all down and decided I would try to make the sauce during the summer in France, since my mother had somehow managed to buy a modest place in the village of Meschers, about a two-hour drive from Bordeaux. All of her friends from the busking days would come with their children and crowd into the house.

I have continued to cook that pasta sauce every summer since. We still go to that same house every summer—my mom, my kids, my brother—and I make variations of it. I never had the actual recipe, so I've been playing around with it from the start.

For a while, I thought I would end up becoming a chef. But I came to the realization that what really made me happy wasn't cooking for people I didn't know. I always took the greatest pleasure in being at home and feeding my friends and family. Most of all, I liked putting in the work that would inspire everyone to sit around the table and spend time together.

The Restaurant That Changed Everything

One day in the spring of 2005, I quit my part-time job at a coffee shop so I could focus on my final exams at school. I was broke. That same day, I became more broke by buying a pair of shoes and some jeans while hanging out with my friends. When I got home and laid the purchases on the bed to admire them, I got a phone call from a number I couldn't recognize. On the other line was a Swedish man. He asked if I could come work at a restaurant called Noma in a few hours.

I had no idea what Noma was. But while I was on the phone with this mysterious man, I noticed that my oldest friend from elementary school, Louisa, was trying nonstop to get through to me. I then remembered that she had worked at a place called Mona, so I figured that this must have had something to do with her needing a replacement. I said yes to the Swedish man and then got the full rundown from Louisa right after: Mona was the casual café of a much fancier restaurant in Christianshavn called Noma. Mona had lasted only a few years, since it was hard to make it run in the colder months of the year (much of it was outdoors). They had already called Louisa to see if she could give some extra help on this night that they were severely understaffed,

but she couldn't and gave them my number. That's how it started.

When I arrived on the wharf in Christianshavn and got to the doorway of the restaurant, I was instantly overwhelmed. I felt out of place. But I took two deep breaths, entered the dining room, and reported for duty. Everyone went out of their way to welcome me, but the place and its energy took over all of my senses. I had never seen anything like it. Watching the level of care and effort was intimidating to someone like me, whose "finest" dining experiences were occasional €20 set menus around France.

I went straight to work. That night I was to pour water, arrange cutlery, and serve bread. I found it so silly to have to keep track of who was drank still and who drank sparkling, and the need for me to make sure no one's glass was ever empty. Why couldn't they leave a few bottles on the table and let the guests do it for themselves?! Still, it was my job, and I did it as best I could.

It was enough for Pontus, the Swedish man who had cold-called me, to ask if I could do it all over again the following day. I said yes, because I was transfixed by everything, even though I couldn't process all that I had seen and heard that shift: total precision, like what I would imagine an opera being like; chefs serving guests, talking about how they pick weeds for the menu out in the forest; dish descriptions that I couldn't possibly conjure in my mind. A new world had opened up to me, just like that.

Pontus and a waiter named Lau quickly took me under their wings. They answered all of my questions, no matter how silly. Pontus, the head sommelier, would let me try amazing bottles, which helped me reverse some of my very misguided opinions: until Pontus,

I didn't like champagne at all—it was either too sour or too sweet, and it always had a corky taste to it. I could barely drink white wine, since I had gotten sick too many times drinking boxed brands when I was fifteen. It was so bad that whenever I tried to drink it, I would have to stop breathing through my nose when I put the glass to my lips. But with this new crew of people, I found myself quickly sniffing and swirling, trying to figure out exactly what I enjoyed the most.

These little revelations kept coming. One of Lau's favorite stories has to do with the end of one of my earliest shifts, when we were all setting up the tables for the next day's lunch service. My task here was to place the butter knife on top of the little bread plate parallel to the base plate, in a vertical line. I thought that I had done a great job of it until suddenly I heard Lau shout, "Who was in charge of arranging the butter knives?!" I quickly came forward, and he told me how they weren't quite parallel enough. He went around the dining room adjusting each of them about one or two millimeters. As he was doing this, I couldn't help but blurt out, "How much could you possibly give a crap about that?! It's not even noticeable!" But it did matter. That was Noma.

Meeting René

After summer break, I called Pontus and told him I wanted to take on as many shifts as possible. That first day back, I was overwhelmed again by the sights and sounds and smells I had encountered only there. I changed into the uniform and someone asked me to head upstairs to grab some linens. I asked where the linens were, exactly, and one of the cooks, who introduced

himself as René, said he could show me. We got in the elevator and I felt an awkward silence—I'm not sure there was one, but I did sense something for about two seconds. I asked what I always asked people when I met them for the first time at Noma: "Sooo, how long have you worked here?" With a half-smile, he looked at me and said from the very beginning, since it was his restaurant. I think I blushed a bit. I thanked him for showing me the linens and thought that he looked pretty young for someone who had his own restaurant.

I had of course seen René around and gotten the sense that he was running things; I am sure that Pontus had pointed him out to me on one of my first shifts. But it was all so much to process that in that moment, it had slipped my mind.

A month and many more shifts later and we were at a staff party at a restaurant called Hurtigkarl, about forty minutes outside of Copenhagen. I felt so lucky to have been invited. It was, by the far, the greatest dining experience I had ever had. It was bliss. After the dinner, we all went to a classic dive in town called Andy's, which stays open until the sun comes up. René was of course there. He and I had been trading glances since we met. He was always kind and would ask about my aspirations and see if he could point me in the right direction. It's what he did for lots of members of staff—always trying to see if he could do something to help. But I felt there might be a bit more under the surface.

Toward the end of the night, some people went home, others went to discos, a few went to get shawarmas or whatever they could eat at that hour. Pontus, René, and I stayed at a table at Andy's. We were the only ones left. René and I had been sneakily holding hands under the table. Pontus *finally* went home, and it happened: René and I kissed! We still discuss about who made the first move. What matters is that it happened.

As we got to know each other better, he showed me so much about flavor. Even though I never wanted to cook in a restaurant, he was a gateway to learning about ingredients, about putting things together and creating flavors, about developing your palate. He inspired me to want to make truly wonderful things. He taught me how to follow my intuition: I stopped taking notes from the TV programs and instead chose to simply get inspired by them. I decided that I wouldn't worry about remembering every little thing and instead follow my senses. I was sure—and I still feel this way—that by watching the programs, the info somehow sticks in my brain without me knowing it and then comes out when I am cooking. By tasting, and guessing what the different ingredients in the dishes are, the combinations of ingredients will also subconsciously stick.

Together we began trying amazing restaurants around the world, which made me want to cook even more at home. From the beginning, among the greatest things he liked about me (and there were many things, of course) was that I would cook every night, even if it was just for me. I got so much pleasure out of it. I would call him during his short break between lunch and din-

ner service to ask him exactly how I should cook my monkfish, or the baby squid that I wanted try out and which had been inspired by a dish that was on the menu at Noma.

I got pregnant in 2007, and as we were getting ready to have our first daughter, Arwen, I thought long and hard about what kind of mother I wanted to be. One of the most important things, I thought to myself, was that I needed to cook for her all the time. I wanted to be the mom who made the best cookies and birthday cakes in the class. But why stop there? I thought.

I started writing down all of my favorite recipes in a notebook. Before I even had our first daughter, I resolved to start developing a family cookbook, something that could be passed on from generation to generation. I wanted to introduce a new tradition to both sides of the family.

Noma's ascent on the world stage coincided with the birth of Arwen. Things got very busy. René was swarmed. I had to cook, I had to come up with more and more recipes, and I loved it. My mom moved in with us every weekend to help me out with Arwen, and we would have the loveliest meals together at home on the weekends when René finally had a breather.

Arwen has been able to make a perfect vinaigrette since the age of five. And now I'm happy to be able to share that, and all that I've learned, in a family cookbook that goes beyond this one well-fed family.